Your Baby's First Year

Your Baby's First Year

A Guide for Teenage Parents

Jeanne Warren Lindsay, MA, CFCS

Morning Glory Press

Buena Park, California

Your Baby's First Year
is part of a six-book series. Other titles are:

*Your Pregnancy and Newborn Journey:
A Guide for Pregnant Teens*

Nurturing Your Newborn

The Challenge of Toddlers

Discipline from Birth to Three

Teen Dads: Rights, Responsibilities and Joys

Library of Congress Cataloging-in-Publication Data
Lindsay, Jeanne Warren.
    Your baby's first year : a guide for teenage parents / Jeanne
Warren Lindsay. -- Rev. ed.
        p.   cm. -- (Teens parenting)
    Includes bibliographical references (p.   ) and index.
    ISBN 1-932538-04-6 (hbk) -- ISBN 1-932538-03-8 (pbk.)
    1. Teenage parents--United States. 2. Child rearing--United
States. 3. Infants--United States. I. Title. II. Series:
Lindsay, Jeanne Warren.   Teens parenting.
HQ759.64.L57   1998
649'. 122--dc21   98-7746
                                                   CIP

MORNING GLORY PRESS, INC.
6595 San Haroldo Way   Buena Park, CA 90620-3748
714/828-1998   1/888-612-8254
Printed and bound in the United States of America

T 5609

Contents

Preface

Nearly half a million teenagers deliver babies each year in the United States, and many of the fathers of these babies are also teenagers. Yet most parenting books are written as if all parents were adults.

A parent who is still an adolescent is part of two worlds, and these two worlds may be in conflict. A teenage parent's life is quite different from the lives of her/his non-parent peers. It may also be quite different from the young families who delay childbearing until both parents have completed their education and are able to form their own household.

I have worked with hundreds of pregnant and parenting teenagers during the past thirty years. Because our school district provides an infant center to care for their babies, many of these young mothers continue attending school on campus after they deliver. Many have fallen into parenthood accidentally, but it is no accident that many are good parents. They've had help along the way from their families and their community, and, most important, they work hard at their parenting job.

This book is a parenting guide especially designed for teenage parents. A major part of it are the comments and parenting suggestions from young people who are "practicing" parents, teenagers who have children of their own. Some are married, some are single. Whatever their marital status, they are more likely to have money problems than are older parents. Many live with their own parents because of their age and/or lack of money.

Names of parents, their children, and a few personal details have been changed in the quotes in order to protect confidentiality. Parents' and children's ages have not been changed. Their comments are real, and quotes are almost always in the exact words used by the young parent.

Your Baby's First Year is part of a six-book series for pregnant and parenting teens. Other titles are *Your Pregnancy and Newborn Journey* and *Nurturing Your Newborn,* both co-authored by Jean Brunelli, PHN; *Discipline from Birth to Three,* co-authored by Sally McCullough; *The Challenge of Toddlers* and *Teen Dads* by Lindsay.

Chapter 5 of *Your Baby's First Year* is written directly to teen fathers while chapter 6 focuses on the special needs of mothers who parent alone. The rest of the book applies both to single parents and to couples who are parenting together.

Parenting at 15, or even 17, is an extremely difficult task. In fact, parenting at any age is quite a challenge for most of us. I hope this book will help young parents understand a little better the world of babies during that all-important first year of parenting.

Jeanne Warren Lindsay   *January, 2004*

Foreword

I became a father for the first time at age 30. My three children are in their late teens and early twenties now. They offered the many parenting challenges that teens typically present. However, nothing has been more exciting, yet completely terrifying, than that first day we spent at home alone with our firstborn. It all seemed so easy while our family was surrounded by the caring, competent attention of the hospital staff. Their confidence inspired our own. Feeding, diapering, feeding again, consoling, diapering again, and sleeping all seemed so simple. We felt so together and so in control.

Then, we went home.

Almost immediately, the routine that seemed easy and normal in the hospital took on a life of its own. Without the support of the hospital staff, each of those tasks grew huge and loomed ominously over us. The feelings of control and competence we had felt in the hospital were revealed for what they were — mere illusions created by the euphoria of brand-new parenthood. We all knew we were in over our heads. Our son, frustrated by the

failure of his parents to fully comprehend the meaning of his
cries, only cried harder. His mother, still sore and recovering
from the Cesarian childbirth, joined him. Finally, succumbing to
my own exhaustion and failure to achieve the same level of
competence I had felt only a day before, I offered my voice to
complete the trio of cries and sobs.

I realize now that first day alone as parents might not have
been as terrifying if we'd had Jeanne Warren Lindsay's book,
Your Baby's First Year. If I, as a 30-year-old father, had such
difficulty adjusting to the new demands of parenting, how must
it be for a teen mom or teen dad?

Jeanne knows the answer to this question better than anyone
else I know. Drawing upon her years of working with teen
parents and her own experience as a mother, she now offers this
updated version of *Your Baby's First Year.* Written specifically
to teen parents, it nonetheless provides practical, insightful
information for all parents of newborns. Jeanne's love for and
belief in teen moms and dads comes through page after page.
From the easy-reading language, to the honest, personal stories
of adolescent parents, to the carefully selected photographs, to
the loving attention given to the most sensitive issues of teen
parenting, Jeanne keeps the focus on the unique needs of her
youthful audience.

I was surprised when Jeanne asked me to write this foreword
for her book. My first internal response was to say, "Wouldn't it
be better to have a mom write this?" As I more carefully consid-
ered her invitation, I realized that her request simply reflected
Jeanne's belief that dads, regardless of their age and relationship
to their child's mother, are important. She sees dads as having a
far more significant role than that of child support provider. For
dads everywhere, of all ages, I thank her. Certainly her chapter,
"For Dad Only," demonstrates her commitment to father
involvement. However, the implied expectation that dads will

want to be invested fathers is woven throughout her book, and this speaks most clearly of Jeanne's belief in active fathering.

In Carlisle, the little Iowa town in which I live, I've been able to experience again (but from a safer distance), the agony and the ecstasy of new parenthood — in the extreme. Carlisle's Kenny and Bobbi McCaughey, Dad and Mom of the now world-famous McCaughey septuplets, live only about four blocks from our house. Not long ago, on a beautiful early spring day, they took the seven five-month-olds and the one two-year-old out for a stroll. The two four-seat strollers looked like mini-Mack trucks as they slowly moved down the sidewalk. All in one breath I said, "Thank God, it's not me," and "Thank God, they have help with those kids." Over the past few months Carlisle has become one huge extended family for the McCaugheys. Without caring community members to provide assistance with rocking, feeding, diapering, consoling, and sleeping, Kenny and Bobbi would surely be beyond wit's end by now. Instead, they are doing well, and the children are thriving, once again reminding us of the power of extended families.

In the foreword of the first edition of this book, Martha Bullock Lamberts wrote, "Readers have access to a kind of extended family in book format — one that is knowledgeable, and warmly caring." Unlike the McCaugheys, teen parents do not always have the help of extended families. Nonetheless, to an adolescent parent, one child may seem like seven. For this reason, Jeanne Warren Lindsay's *Your Baby's First Year* is a true gift to teen moms and dads.

Tom Klaus, M.S., President
Legacy Resource Group
Carlisle, Iowa

ACKNOWLEDGMENTS

I am grateful to all who made time to read and critique part or all of this edition, and to all those who read the earlier editions. Their comments were invaluable.

Perhaps even more important is the input from teen parents, the young people we interviewed, and whose wisdom is scattered throughout the book. For the first two editions, we quoted more than 100 young parents. For this third edition, twelve more young parents were interviewed. Those providing new quotes include Monique Gabriel, Martha Cruz, Jamyette Morales, Eliana Mendez, Sonia Leandro, Genavieve Macias, Alexis Hernandez, Gladys Medina, and Gloria Villegas. Others are quoted and acknowledged in the other books in the *Teens Parenting* series. We also appreciate the many other teenage parents whose insightful quotes are retained from the earlier editions.

The late David Crawford, teacher in the Teen Parent Program, William Daylor High School, Sacramento, supplied many of the photographs. His models were his wonderful students. For this edition, Carole Blum provided additional photographs, mostly of teen parents and their children attending the Teen Parent Program, Tracy High School, Cerritos, CA.

Tim Rinker is the cover artist, and Steve Lindsay helped design the book. I am grateful for the contributions of all of these talented people.

Nora Simoés helped with the proof-reading and kept Morning Glory Press alive and well during book production time. I thank her for her valuable support.

I'm especially grateful to Bob who continues to be supportive even during those times when the current book seems all important. I think he knows he's even *more* important to me.

Jeanne Lindsay

To the young parents
who share so freely on these pages

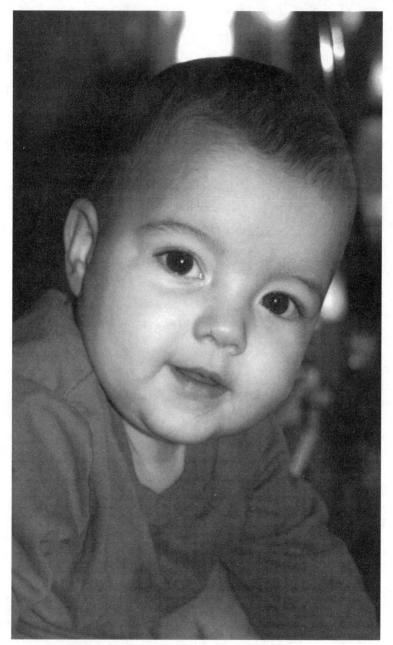

Parenting is indeed a wonderful challenge.

Part I

Those First Months

*If you read **Nurturing Your Newborn**, you learned about parenting during your first three or four weeks with your newborn. There you found suggestions for dealing with crying, bathing your baby, changing diapers, handling your own frustrations. You also read about feeding your newborn, whether by breastfeeding or with bottles.*

*The first chapter of **Your Baby's First Year** will reinforce some of the things you've already learned about your first month with your baby, but in less detail.*

How can one little person change so rapidly in just three or four months? Those amazing changes are discussed in chapter 2, along with the impact you, the parent, have on his physical, emotional, and intellectual development.

You want to help your baby learn as well as possible. Chapter 3 includes a brief discussion of how a person's brain develops and how you can help that development.

You've started the wonderfully challenging journey of parenting. Enjoy!

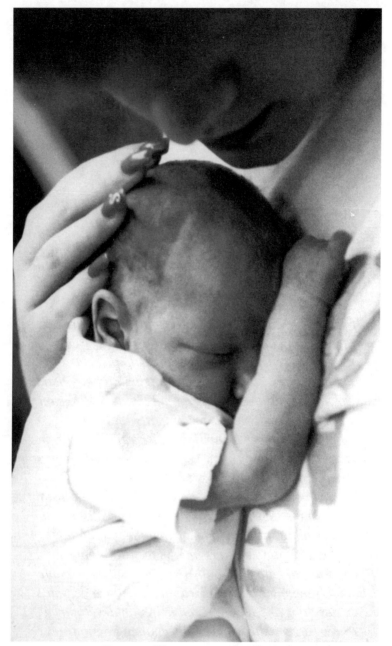

Your new life as a parent has begun.

1

Beginning Life
With Your Baby

*When I first saw her, I couldn't
believe she was mine. I never
saw a newborn before. I started
to cry, and my boyfriend said,
"Why are you crying now?" I
felt something special inside.*

*When I held her for the first
time, I felt like I needed to protect her from everybody. I made
a promise right then that I would
be on her side all the time, that I
would make decisions that would
be best for her even if those
decisions weren't great for me.*

Kimiko, 17 - Sujatha, 5 months

*I couldn't believe she was here,
and that she came out of me.*

Mostly I was happy because now I could take care of her. But I was also scared because I didn't know if I'd be a good mom.

Ukari, 17 - Kendall, 4 weeks

The house was full of people those first two weeks, and that was the worst part of it. I wish they could have waited until a couple of weeks after he was born. I was real tired. It doesn't seem like you ever sleep.

You get home, and he's so tiny you breastfeed every two hours. I was worn out, but my mom cooked for me and kept things clean.

It's funny — nothing would ever wake me up before, but when he makes the slightest cry, I wake up. I'll be in the kitchen, the washer is going, noise everywhere, and I'll hear him.

Adriana, 16 - Danny, 3 months

Never Enough Sleep!

When you come home from the hospital, you will probably be tired, and baby's demands won't give you much time to rest.

Have patience with her. The first couple of weeks I was impatient because I wanted to sleep, and Jenny wouldn't sleep.

Sleep while your baby is sleeping. I had to wash clothes, hang them up, fold them, wash the dishes. You don't have time to sleep, but you have to make time. Sleep was important to me.

Rosita, 18 - Jenny, 4 weeks

Most parents experience this overwhelming tiredness. Most parents also experience the joy of early parenting. Holding your tiny helpless baby is a special and usually wonderful feeling for both mom and dad.

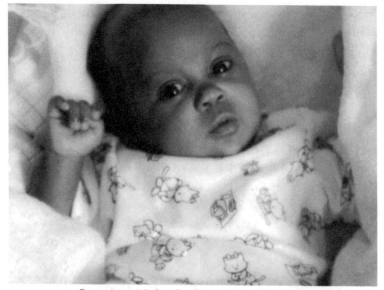

Sometimes it's hard to know what she needs.

Why Do Babies Cry?

The first few months I was having a heart attack because it was all new to me. I'd say, "What's wrong with him? I gave him his bottle. I changed him."

Then I would start crying. I would call my mom or my mother-in-law. I'd get real nervous, but after the first three months, we kind of got the hang of it.

Ernesta 20 - Jeremy, 3; Osvaldo, 5 months

Babies cry for many reasons other than colic. (See page 63 for a discussion of colic.) Most often, she's simply hungry. The solution is also simple. Feed her.

Does your baby need to be burped several times during a feeding? Or is he unhappy if you interrupt his meal to burp him? Perhaps he needs more burping if he cries after you feed him.

Your baby may prefer that you hold him on your shoulder and pat or rub his back until he burps. Or he may like being burped from a sitting position on your lap, or by lying on his stomach across your knees. Your baby may be able to burp in a few seconds, or it could take several minutes. The important point is that he burps when he needs to.

Some babies cry because of a wet or messy diaper. Again, the solution is simple. Change her.

Other babies can't seem to fall asleep without fussing a lot. If you're sure your baby isn't hungry, too cold or too warm, and doesn't need her diaper changed, and she still cries, she may need to be held for awhile.

A ride in the car (safely secured in her car seat) may calm her. Some mothers report their babies fall asleep almost the instant the car starts.

Perhaps she would like some music. She might like soft music beside her crib. Does she have a swing? Sometimes the movement of the swing soothes a baby.

Know that your baby is *not* crying to upset you. She isn't crying because you've spoiled her. Crying is the only way she has to tell you she needs you.

Above all, know that you can *not* spoil an infant. If you are there when she needs you, you're helping her learn to trust her world. She's likely to cry *less* in the future if her needs are met now.

Baby Sets Mealtime

You need to feed your baby whenever he's hungry. That means you *don't* schedule his feeding by the clock. He doesn't have a watch. And he *doesn't* cry to exercise his lungs!

During the first couple of months, most of your baby's crying is probably due to hunger. Offer her your breast or a bottle first. This may be every hour or two at first, especially if you're breastfeeding.

*Patty cries about the average. I don't always feed
her because I can tell if she's hungry. I just pat her on
her back, and she goes back to sleep. She likes a
pacifier, too.*

*I don't let her cry for long. My mom says I should
so she can exercise her lungs, but I don't agree.*

Beth, 18 - Patty, 3 weeks

If she doesn't want food, naturally you don't try to force
her to eat. You look for other reasons for her crying, like
wet or dirty diapers. But first you offer breast or formula.

If You're Breastfeeding

*Why did I breastfeed? Because I feel it's healthier
for the baby, and it's easier instead of making a
bottle. David (teacher) always tells us it's more
nutritious, it helps you have a bond with your baby.
Anybody could feed your baby with a bottle.*

Lacey, 16 - Jenilee, 1 month

Breastfeeding is generally the ideal food for baby. It's
also good for mom — no bottles to clean, no formula to
mix, and it's always the right temperature.

Chapter 11, *Your Pregnancy and Newborn Journey,* and
Chapter 2, *Nurturing Your Newborn,* provide lots of infor-
mation about breastfeeding — why, how, when, and where.
We'll briefly repeat the high points.

First, why breastfeed? It's better for your baby, and can
be extremely satisfying for mom. It's cheaper, and it's
more convenient.

Even if you breastfeed your baby for only a few days,
you'll give him extra protection against illness. Your
breasts don't produce milk for two or three days after
delivery. Instead, they produce colostrum, a yellowish
substance which will help your baby fight off colds and

other illnesses. Those first few days of breastfeeding give your baby a good start in life.

When your nipples are sore, as they may be that first week, letting them air dry after feeding will help. If your baby latches on properly, your nipples shouldn't hurt much. (Latching on refers to baby getting your nipple into his mouth.) Be sure to get as much as possible of the areola (dark area around the nipple) into his mouth as he sucks. If it hurts, break the suction and take him off, then latch him on with more of the areola in his mouth.

Kendall latched on fine at the hospital. It still hurt, but the nurse said it would get better. I'm glad I continued. I told them not to give her bottles, to bring her to me on demand, and they did. No bottles.

Ukari

The more your baby sucks, the more milk your body will produce. To give breastfeeding a good start, it's best not to give baby a bottle during the first month.

Getting enough sleep is harder because my boy-friend can't get up and feed her since I breastfeed. He said he'd wake up and give her a bottle, but since I'm breastfeeding, he can't. Once in awhile, when I'm just too tired, I tell him to make a bottle and give it to her.

Ukari

It's a good idea to offer her a bottle once in awhile after the first month. Then she'll be more willing to take a bottle if you aren't available — and so dad and grandma can feed her occasionally.

It's not necessary to hide in your bedroom while you breastfeed. Babies like to eat when they get hungry, just as we do, only it's much harder for them to wait awhile. You should be able to breastfeed almost anywhere by throwing a blanket over your baby.

> *I think breastfeeding is easier than bottle-feeding.*
> *When the baby wakes up in the middle of the night, I*
> *don't have to get up and heat the bottle. For me, it's*
> *easier to put her to my breast.*
>
> *I started using bottles when I went out because I*
> *didn't want to breastfeed in public. Now I breastfeed*
> *her anywhere because I know how not to expose*
> *myself. Sometimes you need practice.*
>
> Kimiko

Breastfeeding for a Little While

Some mothers breastfeed only the first few days. They
know how important the colostrum is for the baby during
this time. Many moms continue until baby can drink milk
out of a cup, perhaps for a year. Their babies may have an
occasional bottle, but rely mostly on breastfeeding. A few
moms breastfeed longer, and that's certainly okay, too.

> *I breastfed because all my aunts, everyone in my*
> *family always breastfed. They told me if I ever had a*
> *baby, it was best to breastfeed.*
>
> *I breastfed him until he was two. I'd go over to the*
> *Infant Center at his naptime and feed him.*
>
> Mariaeliza, 17 - Joseph, 3

Shauntika breastfed for awhile, then decided to switch to
bottles:

> *I was breastfeeding during the weeks I was out of*
> *school. It was great, but I stopped when I went back*
> *to school.*
>
> *At first it was hard because I didn't know what I*
> *was doing. My breasts hurt after I stopped. I stopped*
> *breastfeeding on Saturday, and he started on the*
> *bottle on Sunday.*
>
> Shauntika, 17 - Dante, 5 months

If you decide to stop breastfeeding your baby, do it gradually. Suddenly switching baby from your breast to a bottle would be hard on both you and your baby.

Shauntika's breasts hurt after she stopped because her body continued producing milk. It's far better to give baby a bottle for one of her feedings each day for a few days, then cut out another breastfeeding, then another, until you're feeding her from the bottle all the time. You'll both adjust to the change much better than if you switch suddenly.

Whether you choose to breastfeed for a few days, a few months, a year, or longer, know that you are giving your baby a wonderful gift that only you can give him.

If You're Bottle-Feeding

If you're bottle-feeding, you probably already know you can choose from ready-to-use, concentrated, or powdered formula. The ready-to-use formula is the most expensive and the easiest to use.

Whichever formula you choose, follow instructions carefully. Be sure bottles and nipples are absolutely clean. Boil the water and let it cool before you mix it with either the concentrated or powdered formula. Always check the temperature of the formula before giving it to baby.

If your bottle-fed baby fusses quite a bit, it's possible he's allergic to cow's milk. Ask your healthcare provider if she needs to prescribe a formula made of soybean powder.

Don't heat your baby's bottle in the microwave oven. This is dangerous. While the bottle may feel cool, the formula inside could be hot enough to burn your baby.

Whether you breast- or bottle-feed, hold your baby close while you feed her. This is a wonderful getting-acquainted time for both of you. As you talk and smile with her, you'll feel even closer to each other.

Mealtime is very special for baby and mom.

Is She Getting Enough?

I pretty much fed him on demand. He was a good baby. He'd get up to eat at night, then go right back to sleep.

My cousin doesn't believe in feeding on demand. She says Orlando will get fat, that he'll be obsessed with food when he gets older. But Orlando knows when to eat.

Holly, 17 - Orlando, 5 months

If you're bottle-feeding, you know how much formula you're giving baby. If baby sometimes doesn't finish his bottle, he probably wasn't as hungry as usual. Don't insist he drink it all. His appetite, just like yours, will vary from feeding to feeding. If he drains his bottle and still seems hungry, he may need more formula now.

Some breastfeeding moms worry because they don't know exactly how much food baby is getting. Is he satisfied for at least an hour or two after each feeding? Is he active when he's awake? Does he have at least 6-8 wet diapers each day? Is he gaining weight? If these things are happening, he's telling you he's getting enough milk.

If your baby seems hungrier at about two weeks, six weeks, and three months, it's probably because she's growing especially fast. She needs more food, and you might not have enough milk for her. The solution is not to stop nursing or to rush for the formula. Instead, simply nurse her more often. Baby controls your supply of milk. She nurses more often, you make more milk. It may take about two days to increase your milk supply. Then she'll probably nurse less often again, and be content.

Especially if you're breastfeeding, your baby doesn't need water the first four to six months.

If he has a fever or diarrhea, however, he needs extra water. If baby has the hiccups, offer him a sip of water from a teaspoon. By the time he's four months old, you can try giving baby a little water from a small cup. He may be ready to take a couple of tiny sips.

No Propped Bottles — Ever

I don't like bottle propping. Babies choke. They drink it too fast, and they can't swallow it.

Chelsea, 19 - Clancy, 2 months

Always hold baby when you give him a bottle. Laying him down and propping his bottle in his mouth is *not* a good thing to do.

A propped bottle gives him no love or emotional support. He needs that from you. He needs eye contact while he's eating.

In addition to the loving he gets from being held while he eats, he's also less likely to have an ear infection if you don't ever prop his bottle. Many ear infections are caused by baby drinking from a propped bottle. The passageway from the ear to the throat doesn't drain well in infancy. Formula, if not "served" properly, can go back to his ears and cause an infection.

Drinking from a propped bottle is dangerous in another way for baby. If he spits up, he could choke on the milk curd because he'd be unable to spit it out with a bottle propped in his mouth.

Even when he's old enough to hold his own bottle, continuing to hold him as you feed him is comforting for both of you. Moving from the bottle to a cup will probably be easier for baby, too, if he isn't used to carrying his bottle around with him.

If your baby needs more sucking than she gets from your breast or the bottle, she may need a pacifier. You don't want to give her a pacifier when she needs to be fed, but it's absolutely okay to offer a pacifier after a feeding.

Just don't substitute the pacifier for the attention, food, or diaper change she wants and needs when she's crying.

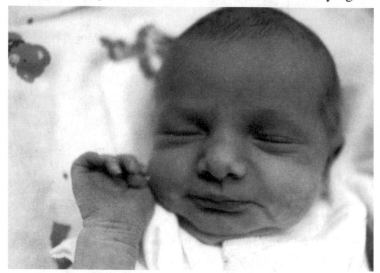

He's sleeping soundly — but soon he'll be ready to eat again.

Bathing Your Baby

We know baby wants to be comfortable. To be comfortable, she needs to be kept clean.

You probably gave your baby "sponge" baths during his first week or two at home. You didn't put him in the water until his navel cord dropped off. You probably laid him on a towel in a warm room, washed him with a soapy washcloth, rinsed him thoroughly, and dried him.

Those real baths, when you set baby in the water, can be a little scary at first.

My mother gave Orlando his first bath. She offered for me to do it, but I let her the first two times. I was totally scared when I first bathed him. I would cry because he cried. I think he didn't like to be naked at first, but now he loves it.

Holly, 17 - Orlando, 5 months

When you bathe baby, wash his head and face first. Don't use soap on his face. Wash his hair with plain soap or baby shampoo at least once a week. Then use your hand to lather the rest of his body with plain soap. Wash his genitals just as you do the rest of his body. After rinsing him thoroughly, wrap him in a towel and pat him dry.

A lot of girls are scared to hold the baby because he's too slippery. He's little, but he's a person, too, and you shouldn't be afraid of holding him.

Gary likes his bath now, and he laughs a little when I wash his hair with warm water.

Leica, 18 - Gary, 3 months

Bathtime is a great time to talk with baby. Describe what you're doing. Tell him how gorgeous he is. He may not like his bath at first, but he'll probably enjoy it before long.

When you bathe baby, *always* test the water to be sure it isn't too hot. Stick your elbow in it. It's more sensitive to temperature than your hands are.

Never leave baby alone in her bath.

Vitamin/Mineral Supplements

You need to continue taking your prenatal vitamins for at least two or three months if you're breastfeeding. Because you're taking vitamins, your baby won't need an extra vitamin supplement during those first months. She's getting her vitamins from your milk.

Have you asked your doctor if baby needs extra fluoride? Getting enough fluoride helps prevent cavities in our teeth, while too much fluoride can be a problem. It can lead to discolored teeth.

Since the amount of fluoride in your water supply may be high or low, it's important that you ask your healthcare provider how much, if any, fluoride supplement your baby needs. Give exactly as prescribed. Don't overdose!

Iron. If you're eating enough nutritious, iron-rich foods, your breast milk will provide enough iron for your baby for about four months. At that time, your healthcare provider may suggest an iron supplement. Or she may tell you it's all right to start feeding baby an iron-fortified cereal.

Most commercial formulas contain iron. Your doctor will help you decide which one is best for your baby.

Taking Care of You

Taking care of a baby is a lot tougher than I thought. I'd been baby-sitting before and I liked it, but it's harder when it's your kid. He's constantly on my mind. I think of nothing else.

I wake up, "Is he okay?" When I go to sleep I have to hear him breathing. When I was baby-sitting, I'd

feed them and take care of them when they were
awake, but I didn't worry so much.

Seilay, 16 - Anders, 3 weeks

How do you handle your own feelings? It's especially
hard if your baby cries a lot. Some babies simply cry more
than others, no matter how much mom and dad try to meet
their needs.

The hardest part of those first weeks with baby may be
lack of time to do *anything* for yourself.

These first weeks, I liked everything, really, except
waking up in the night. I like watching him, feeding
him, taking care of him.

I don't like that I don't have time to do what I need
to do. I still need to clean, take a shower. When he
goes to sleep, I only have a two-hour period, and I'm
cleaning my room, taking a shower, everything.
Sometimes I take a nap. I used to be half asleep trying
to give him a bottle, but now I'm used to it.

Seilay

Whether you're breastfeeding or bottle-feeding, you
need to take good care of yourself. When you're
breastfeeding, you need about 500 extra calories each day.
A sandwich and two extra glasses of milk in addition to
your "regular" nutritious diet should be enough.

Also be sure you drink 12-16 glasses of liquids each day.
You don't have to drink milk to make breastmilk. Of
course if you can drink milk, include it as part of your
liquids. In addition, drink water and fruit juices,

If you drink coffee, tea, or soft drinks, limit yourself to
two cups each day. Choose decaf versions because
caffeinated beverages are not good for your baby.

When you're nursing, get comfortable. If you get too
tired, you may not be able to produce as much milk. Even if

you're bottle-feeding, your baby doesn't need an exhausted mother. *Take care of yourself.*

If you can get back to school three or four weeks after baby is born, preferably with baby, you'll be terribly busy. But you may find this actually reduces your frustrations.

> *The Teen Parent Program is a big help for me. I was worried about getting home study and being in the house the whole day. For me, having the infant center and the school is like a break from everything. I never had time for myself until I started school. I took her to the bathroom with me the first two months. Those first two months were difficult.*
>
> Kimiko

She's Changing Rapidly

> *Anders was all wrinkly at first, but now he has gotten bigger, and he's filled out.*
>
> Seilay, 16 - Anders, 3 weeks

Talk to your baby whenever she's awake. Your baby is changing rapidly even during her first month on the outside. As each week passes, she will respond more and more to your conversation. You, her parent, are the most important person in her world.

Feeding your baby, whether by breast or bottle, is an important part of keeping her comfortable. Each mealtime is a special time of closeness, warmth, and love as you talk and gaze into each other's eyes.

As we've stressed before, feed him when he's hungry. Change him when he's wet. Talk to him and hold him when he's lonely. He'll reward you by responding to you more and more as the days go by.

Your journey through parenthood has begun.

Putting things in his mouth is his way of finding out more about them.

2

His World Changes

*Juan tries to talk back to me, and
he makes noises. He's usually
happy and has a big smile. He
laughs out loud.*

*He sleeps through the night.
When he woke up in the morning,
he used to cry right away. Now he
plays awhile until I wake up. He
sleeps with a bear, and when he
wakes up, he talks to it. He goes
all over the place on his bed,
turning back and forth.*

*Picking him up before, he was
just there, but now he has a lot of
personality. He loves his bath —
even likes his hair washed. It
makes him tired, ready to sleep.*

Ginny, 17 - Juan, 4 months

How Is He Changing?

By the time he's two months old, baby's world *and yours* is changing rapidly. By the time he's four months old, that usually sleepy infant turns into a little person who can "do something."

As a starter, your baby's control of his head will change rapidly. At birth, he has little control over that heavy head. He needs you to support his head when you lift and hold him. A month later, he still needs his head supported. If you put him on his tummy, however, he can now lift his head a little and turn it from side to side. By two months, he can lift it up and keep it up for a few seconds.

When he's three months old, his neck and upper back muscles have grown stronger. On his tummy, he can prop himself on his arms and hold his head up. If you pick him up when he's lying on his back, his head should no longer fall backward as you lift him. Compared to his skills in this area at birth, he has improved remarkably.

He's Smiling Now

Perhaps the most exciting thing a two-month-old does is smile. If she feels good, she'll smile at almost anyone.

Four months is an especially popular age for taking pictures for sending to grandparents. You can almost depend on baby to smile and look great while you're clicking the camera. By this time, too, she will probably be giggling and laughing out loud.

About a week ago Gary discovered his feet. He pulls on them, tries to stick them in his mouth. He coos, yells, screams all the time.

He's starting to laugh out loud now. He's happy all the time except when he's wet or hungry.

Leica, 18 - Gary, 3 months

Hands Are Big Discovery

*At about four months she started looking at her
hands. She'd move them around and stare at them for
the longest time.*

Shuquala, 17 - Haley, 9 months

By three or four months, a big and important change
occurs when your baby starts looking at her hands.
Sometimes this is called "hand regard."

The first month or so, her hands are fisted, and she
doesn't seem to be aware of them. She puts her fist in her
mouth and sucks on it soon after birth, but this is more a
reflex action, not a learned activity. If you put your finger
in her fist, you will be amazed at the strength of her grip,
but again, this is a reflex action.

By two months, she will follow moving objects with her
eyes. Her hand will open and close as she uses her whole
arm to reach for an object.

Put a toy in her hand so she can feel it and watch it as
she moves her arm.

Within another month, she may hold one hand in front of
her face and stare at it, sometimes for several minutes.

*Carol sticks her hands in her mouth, looks at them,
clasps them on her stomach. Yesterday she looked
down and got almost bug-eyed staring at her hand.*

Kristyn, 17 - Carol, 3 months

She looks at her hands now partly because she can see
them more clearly. During her first month or two of life,
she couldn't see small nearby objects very well. The world
was a little hazy for her. By the time she's three or four
months old, she probably sees about as well as any adult.

As her hands become less and less fisted, she will be
able to move her fingers. This gives her something more to

study. You may see her staring at her hands, moving her
fingers back and forth, for five to ten minutes at a time.

A week or two after baby starts staring at her hands, she
may begin to bat at objects. Hold a rattle five or six inches
from her eyes. She will probably not only look at it, but she
may also raise her fist and try to hit it.

Lots of Changes

*Carol scoots. Sometimes I put her down on one
side of the blanket. When I go put clothes in the dryer,
she's off the blanket when I come back.*

*She rolls over both from back to stomach and the
other way. We help her with pillows. She can sit up
for a second, then she falls back down.*

Kristyn

This stage is the last time your baby will spend most of
his time on his back or on his stomach. He will soon learn
to turn over from back to stomach and from stomach
to back.

He's probably awake about half the time now, and he
may seem happy much of the time. Illness, indigestion, and
cutting teeth, of course, can cause unhappiness. Generally,
however, things look good to a two- to four-month-old
individual.

By three or four months, baby can sit up with support.
Sitting upright gives her a much better view of her world.
Think about it. How much could you see if you were
usually lying down? What a difference it makes to be able
to sit up!

*I prop Blair up in the corner of the couch and put
pillows around him. He likes that position. He can see
more. He's curious.*

Brooke, 18 - Blair, 3 months

No Solid Food Yet

Babies under four to six months of age don't need and shouldn't have anything to eat except breast milk or formula. Their digestive systems aren't ready for other foods.

Feeding a two-month-old baby cereal in the evening is not going to help him sleep all night. It may make him cross and fussy the next day because of problems with digestion caused by the cereal. If so, he may be so tired by night that he'll sleep better. But don't give the cereal credit for the sleep.

Rania, 16, mother of Khalid, 2 months, complained that Khalid was crying a lot at night. She also mentioned that she was giving him cereal at night. She said he needed the solid food. The school nurse suggested Rania try putting Khalid to bed without the cereal for a couple of nights. Perhaps he would sleep better.

When Rania came to school a few days later, she pulled me (her teacher) aside, and said, "Ms. Lindsay, you need to tell those girls that they shouldn't give their babies cereal at night. It's hard on their stomachs. Khalid slept much better the past two nights when he didn't get cereal."

Needless to say, it was Rania who told "those girls" about the folly of giving their babies solid food too soon.

Playing with Baby

What is Caelin like now? She smiles more. She recognizes me when I leave the room. Before, she would cry when I left the room, but now she doesn't. She sort of giggles. She moves her hands, and everything I give her she puts in her mouth.

I put a stuffed animal on top of Caelin, and she moves it away. She watches her mobile, and she laughs. She has a little mirror, too, and she laughs at it. And she has this cookie monster. When you hit it, it

She likes to be outdoors.

shakes. So she kicks it because I think she likes the
vibrating.
When I read to Caelin, she smiles and looks at
everything on each page.

Alaina, 17 - Caelin, 4 months

If the weather is pleasant, baby will love going outdoors.
Lay her on a blanket under a tree where she can watch the
sunlight coming through and hear the rustling of the leaves.
Don't leave her outside alone, however, unless you're
working by a window very close to her.

Her first toys need to be big enough for her to hold
easily, yet too big to put in her mouth. Her toys should be
washable with no sharp edges or corners. Remove any parts
that come off easily. Take out the button eyes on her
stuffed animals. You can embroider charming eyes for the
toys, eyes that she can't choke on or swallow.

Helping Her Exercise

I put her up on the couch and prop her so she
won't fall. I exercise her. When I put her on her
stomach she rolls over, first her head, and then her
body. And when I have her on my lap, I stand her up,
and she pushes down with her feet.

Alaina

We all need to exercise, even your baby. Give her plenty
of opportunity to kick her feet and wave her arms freely.
When she's three or four months old, she'll be able to hold
her legs up. If the room is warm enough, she'll especially
enjoy exercising without any clothes on.

When she's on her back, she'll soon start kicking. If she
feels pressure against the soles of her feet, she may push
against this pressure over and over.

You can provide pressure to her feet in two ways. First,
if the end of the crib is solid, place her so she can push
against it with her feet. Second, you can briefly stand her
on a hard surface. She may enjoy pushing down with her
feet for a minute or two.

She would enjoy your help as she exercises. Hold her
feet gently and push her knees up to her stomach a few
times. *Be gentle.*

Hold her hands, or let her grasp your finger. If she's able
to hold her head up, pull her gently to a sitting position. If
her head is still wobbly, wait awhile for this one.

Help her roll from side to side on the bed. Gently
massage her legs, arms, and body. She'll love it.

He Needs a Peaceful Home

In addition to simple comfort, baby prefers a generally
peaceful home. If her parents argue a lot, she will sense it.
She may become as upset as they are.

One young mother described her first month with her baby. She lived with the baby's father, and their relationship was not going well.

The baby cried a great deal which proved to be the breaking point in his parents' relationship. Kimberly was so tired from caring for little Karl that she had no time left for Tom. She also resented the fact that he refused to help her take care of their baby. Tom, in turn, felt left out and generally unhappy. One night they had another terrible argument. Kimberly decided to take Karl and move back with her mother:

> *I stayed with Tom for two more days, but we weren't speaking. Karl was upset the whole time. In fact, he cried a lot from the day we came home from the hospital.*
>
> *As soon as we moved in with my mother, Karl began sleeping through the night. He's been an entirely different baby. Instead of crying all the time, he's smiling at us now. I know all that arguing was hard on him. I'm glad I finally found the courage to leave.*
>
> Kimberly, 17 - Karl, 2 months

Ideally, both mom and dad are involved with baby. It's possible that in time Kimberly and Tom will be able to parent together — or they may not. At this time, Kimberly decided their relationship simply wasn't working.

When parents are having a hard time with their relationship, only they can decide if continuing that relationship is the best decision for them and for their baby. Sometimes talking with a marriage/relationship counselor can help. If one parent refuses to see the counselor, the other parent may gain insight into their difficulties by going to counseling alone.

The parents' relationship difficulties certainly can affect their baby. If these problems can be worked out, it's better for baby.

Other Caregivers

Some parents stay home most of the time with their newborn baby. Especially if she's breastfeeding, mother may find it easier as well as more pleasant for both herself and the baby if she doesn't try to take him out much or attempt to leave without him during those first weeks.

By two months, however, you'll want to go out, do things on your own occasionally. Unless you have a live-in sitter, you'll need to let your sitter know where baby's things are kept and the style of care baby needs. Does he expect rocking after feeding? Is he hard to burp? Does he whimper a few minutes before falling asleep?

In addition, be sure to leave phone numbers for your doctor, a caring neighbor, the fire department, and the police department. Put the numbers where the sitter can find them easily. Always let him/her know exactly how to reach you while you're gone.

Some parents leave Medicaid stickers with a sitter if they're going to be gone long.

Whenever you leave your child with someone else, it's wise to give that person a signed medical emergency card. You could state, "_____ *has my permission to obtain emergency medical care as needed for my child."* Be sure you sign the card. Generally, medical care may not be given to a child without the parent's permission.

What About Family Planning?

Another baby? Not for a long time. Maybe when I can offer everything the baby needs. It's hard enough with one.

Two would be a lot harder. Then I'd really have
trouble taking my shower! I don't know how people
do it, taking care of two.

                        Seilay, 16 - Anders, 3 weeks

Couples need to think and talk about future family plans.
How soon do you want another child? Many young mothers, married as well as single, don't want another baby right
away. From a physical standpoint, their bodies need time to
recuperate from the last pregnancy.

Breastfeeding won't keep you from getting pregnant.
You conceive *before* a menstrual period. Even if you
haven't had a period since you delivered, you can get
pregnant.

Another baby? Not very soon. We want to wait
three or four years. We're pretty careful with contra-
ception because we don't want another baby right
away.

That would be hard because we'd be spending
twice as much on diapers and everything else. It
would make everything harder.

It'll also be easier when Keegan is 3 or 4 years old
because he'll know more. He won't cry as much.
We've agreed to wait.

                        Randy, 17 - Keegan, 2 months

See chapter 15 for more comments from young parents
on this issue. Also see chapter 14, *Your Pregnancy and
Newborn Journey,* for more information on family
planning methods.

Babies often come by accident. If you don't want to get
pregnant again soon, you and your partner need to discuss
your prevention plan. You either need to abstain totally
from sexual intercourse, or you need to use contraception
every time.

*I don't want the next one until I'm settled down and
I know what I'm doing. It's going to be hard enough
with one baby. Why would I want to bring another
baby into the world if it's going to be that hard?*

Ukari, 17 - Kendall, 4 weeks

Your healthcare provider will want to see you four to six
weeks after your baby is born. Be *sure* to keep this appoint-
ment. She will check your health and make sure you're
recovering well from pregnancy and delivery. If you
haven't already talked with her about birth control, this is a
good time to do so.

Call WIC for Food Expense Help

Perhaps it's hard for you to get enough of the right foods
for yourself while you're breastfeeding. Call your Public
Health Department for information about WIC (Special
Supplemental Feeding Program for Women, Infants, and
Children). You may be able to get coupons for certain
foods you need. In many communities, the fact that you're
a teenage mother may make you eligible for help from
WIC.

WIC also provides help in buying nutritious foods for
pregnant women and for baby's formula.

The food stamp program helps extend food dollars for
eligible families. Ask your social worker for information.

No Longer a Newborn

Your newborn changes more rapidly during these first
four months than he ever will again. These first months
offer a real challenge to baby's parents. Your major task is
simply to meet his needs as much as possible.

Love him, keep him comfortable, play with him, talk to
him *often*, and enjoy him.

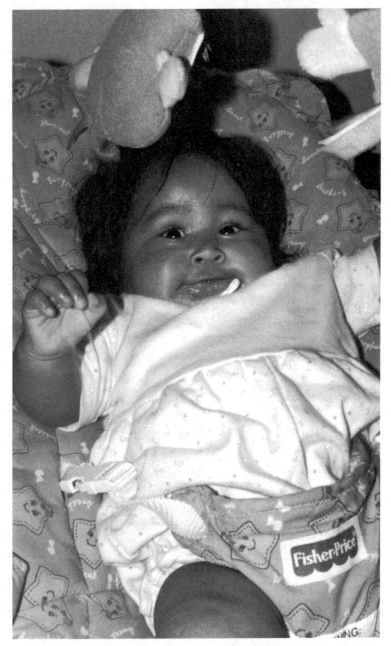

She's ready and eager to learn.

3

Building Baby's Brainpower

I read to Buchanan and he loves it. He stares at me like he understands what I'm saying. I know he does.

I think reading to him will help him form his speech, plus it's our time together. He sits there all quiet and listens to me. I think he likes the sound of my voice. He looks at the book, and then he looks up at me. He's so cute.

Camelia, 16 - Buchanan, 6 months

Joys the first two months? The first time she smiled, and she started to recognize my voice, started grabbing my fingers.

Kimiko, 17 – Sujatha, 5 months

Helping Baby's Brain Develop

Do you want your child to be bright, to learn easily? A great deal of his future learning ability depends on you.

When your baby was born, the only organ not completely formed was his brain. In fact, a newborn's brain is about one-fourth the size of an adult's brain. Immature as it is, however, his brain already contains millions of neurons (nerve cells). In fact, he already has most of the brain cells he needs. Connecting these cells are trillions of connectors or *synapses*.

However, after birth, she must grow many more of the essential connections/synapses between her brain cells. The "wiring" of her brain is made up of these synapses. Many, many (actually, trillions!) new sypapses are formed during the first three years while others are pruned away (no longer exist).

In fact, by age three, his brain will grow to about 90 percent of the size of an adult brain. In other words, about two-thirds of his brain develops between the time he is born and his third birthday.

Some parts of his brain will not change much after birth. But much of the brain is "plastic" — it's shaped by its surroundings and by repeated experiences. A person's capacity for abstract learning and thinking is particularly plastic. This is where parents can really make a difference.

Your baby's brain is "wired" by his experiences, both negative and positive. When he is born, his actions are controlled by the brainstem, sometimes called the alarm center of the brain. Of course he can't yet reason or engage in abstract thinking. He can't control his emotions at first. It's important that his basic needs are met, combined with lots of close contact (cuddling, talking, singing) with you.

The *limbic,* or emotional part of her brain develops most

rapidly during the first year. The *cortex*, the logical part of the brain, is mostly inactive at birth, but is more developed by the end of her first year.

Importance of Responding Quickly

How you respond to your baby has a great deal to do with his ability to learn, relate to people, and manage his emotions. How quickly do you respond to your baby's needs? Can you tell when he's hungry before he starts real crying? Some babies let mom know they're hungry before they start crying. Observe your baby closely. As you become more and more comfortable with each other, you'll be able to respond quickly to his needs.

When your baby learns very early that she can depend on you and her other caregivers to meet her needs, she will build the all-important feeling of security. If she feels secure that these needs will continue to be met, she can place her attention on exploring the rest of her world. She can allow her brain to grow to take in all these wonders. Do *NOT* worry about spoiling her during these early months!

My grandmother is afraid I'll spoil her because when Jenilee cries, I pick her up. I believe she cries for a reason, and that you can't spoil a newborn, so I don't really pay attention to Grandma.

When Jenilee cries, I pick her up and hold her against my chest with her face where she can hear my heart beat. Or I walk her while I'm standing up. She likes me to walk around with her. Or I start talking with her. She likes to listen to my voice.

Lacey, 16 - Jenilee, 1 month

If your baby is happy, if he hears lots of music and speech, he gets lots of hugs and eye contact, all of these things actually change the physiological development of his brain. The quality and quantity of the electrical wiring between his brain cells depend on these actions with a caregiver. We know that the better a baby's brain is wired, the better his life will be.

So your child's most rapid brain growth happens in her first three years. By the time she is 2, in fact, her brain has twice as many synapses as an adult's. This early growth spurt is complete by age 10. Synapses that have not been stimulated die off.

Parents' Role in Baby's Brain Development

Your baby's early experiences have a huge effect on the development of these synapses. You have probably heard the phrase, "Use it or lose it." Well, this applies strongly to your baby's brain development. When you cuddle your baby, you're stimulating his brain development. Talking with him, reading, singing to him cause more synapses to form.

Babies who don't get enough attention, whose caregivers don't respond to their needs promptly, will develop fewer of these learning paths in their brains.

It's during your child's first three years that these connections in the brain are made permanent. Because of outside experiences, changes in one's brain continue as the individual matures. However, as mentioned before, the most rapid changes occur in the first three years of life. Everything is new to a child, so of course he has more to learn during this time than he ever will again.

As your child's parent, you are the most important designer of your child's learning experiences, experiences which will cause those synapses to develop.

If you love your baby a lot and respond to her cries for food, warmth, dryness, cuddling, and sleep, she will probably do well during her first six to eight months. In

Reading with Mom or Dad enriches his life — and his brain.

addition, it's important to read, sing, talk, and play with your child. Your reading, singing, talking and playing with her will have a major impact on her brain development.

Most of the chapters in this book focus on interacting with your baby. Over and over you'll read about the importance of talking and reading to your baby, and of providing the care and stimulation he needs.

This chapter is designed to help you understand how all these things will help your baby develop into a bright and happy individual. Here, the emphasis is on helping baby's brain develop during the first few months after birth. Chapter 11, "Playing with Your Baby," includes many suggestions for enriching experiences for your child during his second four-month stage. In chapter 14, "Enjoying / Teaching Your Child," the focus is on teaching your child during the last four months of his first year.

This is an important year for your baby, and for his brain development.

Newborns and the Power of Touch

Your baby first became aware of your love through your touch. Touching actually sends signals to the brain telling it how to make those necessary connections.

Research has shown that when premature infants are gently massaged, they grow faster and are calmer. Massage helps babies develop movement earlier, sleep more soundly, and have less colic.

When your baby was in your uterus, she was "massaged" much of the time as you moved about. The massaging needs to continue after birth. Scientists tell us that touch is as crucial a "nutrient" as vitamins!

So cuddle your baby. Hold him. Gently massage his arms, legs, and body. A chest carrier is good for a tiny baby. In it, he can be close to mother or dad. Lying for long periods in an infant carrier is not nearly as nice for him. Being close to mom or dad at this stage helps those synapses form.

One thing that really bothers me is when people take their baby around in the carrier. Why can't they hold them? It's so important that babies be held when they're littler. I can see if they're sleeping, but if the baby is wide awake, they put them in it, and set it in front of the TV. That doesn't make sense.

Aimee, 17 - Amelia, 10 months

A baby carrier is convenient during this stage. If you're not holding baby, and she's not sleeping in her crib, it allows her to see more than when she's lying flat. But it's *not* a substitute for arms.

Your baby is likely to prefer being in a sturdy sling carrier on your chest over something you hold at arm's length away from you. Wouldn't you? She can be close to you even when you're using your hands for other activities.

Note: When your baby is riding in the car, of course, he *must* be in a sturdy car seat in the back facing the rear of the car. Being in your arms while he's riding is *not* safe for him.

Conversations with Baby

Someone may tell you that a newborn does not react to another person. Don't believe it! You have probably already discovered that your baby responds when you talk or sing to her. From the day she is born, she *needs* talking and singing in addition to having her physical needs for food, warmth, and comfort satisfied.

At first I wondered, how am I going to talk to her? What will I say? She probably won't even know. But after my mom told me to talk to her, and that it's good for them, I started talking to her.

Adia, 17 - Shareef, 11 months

At this early stage, your baby can't yet form words. He probably won't be saying more than a few words by his first birthday. Long before this, however, his hearing system is being developed by the things you and others say to him.

So talk to your baby from the day she's born. Tell her how much you love her, how thrilled you are that she is part of your family. Tell her about the people around her, about the weather. Perhaps you'll even tell her about what you learned at school today. Remember, it's the sound of your voice that she likes and needs.

He only cries if he gets hungry, or sometimes if you're not talking to him and he feels lonely, he'll holler out.

He will go to sleep when I go to sleep. When I close
my eyes, he will coo for a little while, and then he
goes to sleep, too.

Brooke, 18 – Blair, 3 months

Eye contact is important for you and your new baby. A
newborn sees you best when you're 9-12" away. Feeding
time is ideal for lots of eye contact between you. By two
months she may respond more if you open your eyes wide
and move your mouth. Or move your head slowly from
side to side, or up and down. See if she can follow the
movement with her eyes.

He *Enjoys* and *Needs* Your Singing

It's also important that you sing to him. At first he will
prefer soft lullabies. Your voice, whether or not you can
"carry a tune," is most precious to him.

Don't be embarrassed if you think your singing is off
key. He doesn't care. He simply loves the sound of your
voice.

Soft recorded music is nice for tiny babies, too. Research
has shown that no particular composer is most preferred.
You might choose classical music, soft popular melodies,
or low-key "oldies."

As the weeks and months go by, baby will become more
and more responsive to music. You can hold him and
gently rock him in time to the music. Soon you'll be
dancing with him.

All along, you'll know that music now is helping his
brain develop so that he will actually be able to learn more
and become a more capable person as an adult. For example, scientists tell us that children exposed to music
from birth may be better math students later than children
without music in their lives.

Reading to Your Newborn

Over and over in this book you're reminded of the tremendous importance of reading to your child often. Start reading when he's born — or before:

> *When I was pregnant I'd put earphones on my belly and read to her, and she would kick.*
>
> Shaquala, 17 – Haley, 9 months

> *I read to her every night. I started when she was two weeks old. Now she looks at the pictures, and if I turn the page too fast, she cries, and wants the picture back.*
>
> Adia

Reading to your child will have a big impact on her life. The more you read to her, the more synapses will be formed in her brain. At some point, your child will probably want the same book read to her over and over again. When she hears a picture book many times, it helps her begin to understand the connection between the written page and the spoken word.

One study showed that only 50 percent of infants and toddlers have parents who read to them regularly. Not reading to one's child means that child is at risk of not learning as she should. She may not become as capable and intelligent as she could have been.

Bedtime is a favorite reading time in many families. This often leads to the child being able to fall asleep more easily.

Incidentally, there is a strong tie between the amount of sleep a child gets and his brain development. The brain needs to have a period of deep sleep in order to process the experiences of the day. It's a little like processing the information in your computer by downloading it. Children between birth and age 12 who don't get enough sleep don't do well on performance testing, creativity, and higher-level thinking. So talk, sing, read to your child — and encourage him to get plenty of sleep. His brain will thank you.

Make Her Surroundings Interesting

Cuddling, talking, and singing to your baby comes first. As she develops, she also needs a stimulating environment. She is already alert and ready to learn. At this point, it's up to you to make her life interesting. During the first weeks, give her something to look at when she wakes up in her crib.

Soon you'll be playing with her. You'll provide things she can touch and feel, toys that make sounds, bright colors to look at.

Juan likes to feel and chew on things. He knows different textures, and if it's coarse, he doesn't like to hang on to it. He likes his little bunny and dog because they're soft.

Ginny, 17 - Juan, 4 months

From two to six months, the part of your baby's brain that helps him manage his emotions is developing. He begins to enjoy being around people.

She wants to be around a lot of people. She wants to get all the attention. If I don't talk to her, she gets mad. I feel bad seeing a baby cry. If I see my daughter screaming, I grab her.

Kimiko

She is learning that smiling and cooing, as well as crying or fussiness, cause emotional reactions from her caregivers. She is also beginning to learn that she has some control over her emotions.

If you're sensitive to his reactions, you'll realize when he gets tired of an activity. If you're talking to him, or showing him a toy, after a few minutes he may look away. He may be telling you he's not interested right now. Then it's a good idea to stop and change activities. His attention span is still very short.

Value of New Experiences

When you're bored, do you think you're learning much? Probably not. Bored babies aren't learning much either. Even an infant may need a change in scenery. This could be

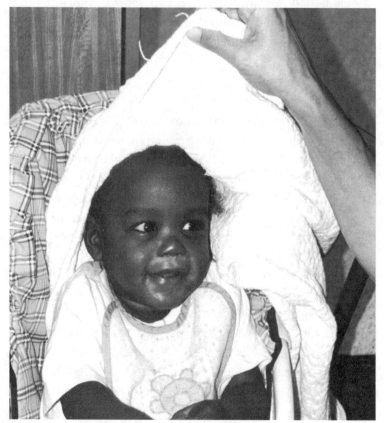

He loves to play peek-a-boo.

simply moving to a different part of the room. Or take him outside if weather permits. Walk around your yard for a few minutes.

She likes to go outside to play. I always took her for walks when she was a month or two old. Now she loves being outdoors.

Adia

Play peek-a-boo over and over with your baby. Sometimes you can vanish behind his blanket, and sometimes he'll be the one who hides. He'll love the game. Over time, it may help him learn that when you vanish, you come back. This may help when you need to leave him with someone else for a while.

Each Baby Is Unique

If you've been around babies, you know how different each one is from the others. They develop at different rates in different ways. Some are very active, some are quiet.

Too often parents and other people think the quiet baby is the "good" baby. In fact, the quiet baby may need more from you than does the very active baby. She needs more stimulation to help her learn about her world because she's not likely to do as much active exploring on her own.

Being "at risk" means the desired behavior/learning will not happen automatically. Much learning at this stage occurs because she is copying your example. Unless you help her, she may not talk as well as she might. Unless you guide her in learning to get along with people, her social development won't be as good as it should be. How you respond to her needs today has a great deal to do with the development of her brain and of the person she becomes.

You have a wonderful responsibility!

Part II
Health Care
and Family

*Your baby's health depends greatly on you, his parent.
You're responsible for making and keeping appointments
for well-baby check-ups, and for scheduling his immunizations. It's you who will care for him when he's ill, and call
his healthcare provider when necessary.*

*In the next chapter you will find tips for keeping your
baby healthy, and for caring for him when he's ill.*

*Families are important to babies. Is Dad involved?
Chapter 5 is written especially to him. Or are you, the
mom, parenting alone? Perhaps you'll find guidance in
chapter 6.*

*Most of us also have extended family. Especially if
you're living with your parents or your partner's parents,
you'll be interested in chapter 7, "Three-Generation
Living."*

Mommy's arms help when baby isn't feeling well.

4

Health Care for Your Baby

Dante has a cold now. I get scared because last time he got sick he had the stomach flu. We had to put him on clear liquids, and give him Pedialyte. That was hard.

When he's sick, you can tell because his eyes look real weak. Now that he has a cold, you can tell because of the snot and the weak eyes, but he still smiles.

Shantika, 17 - Dante, 5 months

Donovan gets sick easy. When he was little, two months old, he had pneumonia, and he was in the hospital for two weeks. I took him to the hospital four times for asthma.

Belia, 17 - Donovan, 2

Working with Healthcare Providers

Your baby's healthcare provider may be a doctor, nurse practitioner, a physician's assistant, or other specialist. In this book, we use both "doctor" and "healthcare provider" to mean health professional.

You probably took your baby to see his healthcare provider when he was about two weeks old, perhaps earlier. You need to continue these periodic checkups throughout the next couple of years.

Each time, before you go in, write down everything you want to discuss. Be sure you ask all your health-related questions. If the doctor is in a hurry, simply tell her, "I have these questions, and I need help." Then briefly describe whatever your worries are. The doctor will take time to advise you. If she doesn't, perhaps you should look for another doctor who will answer your questions.

Do you know the names of the various people working in the doctor's office? It's a good idea to know the names of the receptionist and the nurse. If you can call them by name when you telephone, you're more likely to get a friendly response.

Have you started a healthcare notebook for your baby? It's important that you do. Be sure to keep your notebook up to date. If you're in a managed care health plan, you may see a different doctor each time you go. With the notebook, you'll communicate better with the doctor. When you're organized, the doctor is likely to react in a positive way because you're obviously a capable young parent. That's better for both you and your baby.

In your health notebook, write down your baby's length and weight at birth. Do this every month during this first year. If you know your baby's blood type, write it down.

Most important is your record of your child's immunizations. This record is required when your child starts school

Also keep track of your child's illnesses. Write down the date and briefly describe his symptoms. This will be a big help for you in providing information to your child's healthcare provider.

You are the case manager for your child's medical needs. Keep your child's health notebook in a safe place where you can always find it. Always take your notebook with you when you take your baby to the doctor.

If your baby was born prematurely or has other special needs, please see chapter 9, *Your Pregnancy and Newborn Journey.* This chapter contains additional healthcare information.

Babies and Colic

Shareef had colic and I didn't know what it was. I took her to ER nearly every other day until the pediatrician told me she probably had colic. She'd be up at night crying and crying, and it was just me to watch her. It was real hard to get up and go to school.

Adia, 17 - Shareef, 11 months

What is colic? There is no known cause. The symptoms include intense crying and screaming, usually in the evening. Baby may continue crying for two hours or longer. Nothing the parent does seems to help for more than a few minutes.

About one in five babies appears to have colic. That is, at two or three weeks of age, the baby starts crying hard for no understandable reason. He may seem to have a stomach-ache and have attacks of crying nearly every evening. His face may suddenly become red; he'll frown, draw up his legs, and scream loudly. When you pick him up to comfort him, he keeps screaming, perhaps for 15 to 20 minutes. Just as he is about to fall asleep, he may start screaming again.

He may pass gas.

No one knows what causes colic. It *doesn't* happen because of something the parent does or doesn't do. It generally comes at about the same time every day. During the rest of the day, the colicky baby will probably be happy, alert, eat well, and gain weight.

If you think your baby may have colic, check with your healthcare provider. Is anything else wrong? If not, make sure baby is not hungry, wet, cold, too hot, or lonely.

If you have a colicky baby, you'll do all you can to soothe him, and to stay sane yourself. During an attack of colic, holding him on his stomach across your knees may comfort him. Sometimes giving him a warm bath helps. There are also some medicines that may help. Ask your doctor.

If you have a partner, grandmother, or friend who will take turns carrying and cuddling baby during these crying spells, by all means let them help.

The good news about colic is that baby will grow out of it by the time he is about three months old. In the meantime, he will be harder to live with because of his colic. Comfort him as best you can, and look forward to the time his colic ends.

When Lance was a baby, he always had to be held. He was colicky, and we walked with him a lot. Then overnight at about four months he changed, and he was the best little baby. He was happy, and he didn't cry much any more. What a change.

                    Celia, 20 - Lance, 18 months; Laurel, 4 years

Dealing with Diaper Rash

Kendall had a diaper rash the first week. We used cornstarch, and she got rid of it pretty quickly.

                              Ukari, 17 - Kendall, 4 weeks

Of course you want to prevent diaper rash as much as possible. You'll need to change your baby's diaper before every feeding during the first couple of months. You'll also need to change him every time he has a bowel movement.

Note: Disposable diapers do a good job of absorbing urine. This can cause a problem. If the diaper doesn't feel wet and you don't change him, the absorbed urine can still irritate baby's skin. Change him regularly!

Your baby's skin may be more sensitive to some brands of disposable diapers. Start with the cheaper ones. Sometimes the more expensive brands are more likely to irritate his skin. He might be allergic to something added to the diapers to make them smell nice.

When your baby starts sleeping through the night, put two diapers on her. You can even triple-diaper if she wets so much that her clothing and bedding are soaked by morning. Using a combination of cloth and disposable diapers would probably work best.

Each time you change your baby, wash her with clean water or wipes. The main cause of diaper rash is the ammonia in the urine coming in contact with air. If she gets a rash, it's even more important to wash her thoroughly each time you change her.

If you have a baby girl, always wipe from front to back to keep germs from getting into her vagina. If you have a boy, clean around his penis and his genitals. If he's not circumcised, don't try to pull the foreskin of his penis back to clean him. It will be several years before the foreskin is loose enough to pull back for cleaning underneath. Just clean the exposed areas.

You can put cornstarch or baby powder on her bottom after you take off her wet diaper, but it isn't necessary. If you use baby powder, don't shake it directly on baby. Instead, put a little in your hand first, then pat it on the

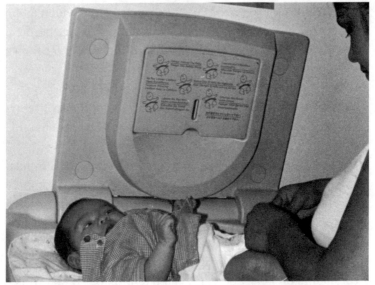

Keeping her clean and dry is important for her comfort.

baby. If you shake baby powder in the air, it can hurt
baby's lungs.

Ask your healthcare provider about prescription and
nonprescription remedies for diaper rash. You can get these
either as powder or ointment. During the day the powder is
better because, each time you change her, you can wash it
off without irritating the rash. At night, however, when
baby will sleep longer, use the ointment. It will give longer
protection.

If your baby develops a bad diaper rash, let her go
without a diaper as much as possible. Air on the rash helps
clear it up. If she's warm enough, she can nap without a
diaper. Of course you'll put an absorbent pad under her,
and protect her bed with waterproof sheeting.

To repeat, it's easier to prevent diaper rash than it is to
get rid of it. For your baby's comfort — and your peace of
mind — change her often. And clean her thoroughly each
time you change her.

Some diaper rashes occur when a baby is taking an antibiotic. Tell your healthcare provider, and she may recommend a special cream to help.

Get Those Immunizations!

Your baby will probably be sick occasionally. He may have a cold, be feverish, or suffer from some other illness. Sometimes you'll need your doctor's help, but these illnesses need not be a big worry. Baby feels lousy and fusses for a few days, but generally he's soon back to normal.

Other childhood diseases can be very serious for your child. The good news is that you can prevent most of these diseases. It's up to you.

Your healthcare provider can immunize him against such diseases as polio, mumps, whooping cough, and measles.

Here's what your child will need:

• **Hepatitis B** is given in a series of three injections. Usually the first is given on baby's first day after birth, the second at one to two months, and the last one at six months. Baby must have all three.

• **Pneumoccal** is given soon after birth. It protects the baby from pneumonia.

• **Diphtheria, Tetanus, Pertussis (DTaP)** is also given in a series of three at 2, 4, and 6 months with a booster (Td) at 15-18 months.

• **H. influenzae, type b (Hib)** is another series of three. This is often given in the same injection as the DTaP and is then called HDTaP.

• **Polio (IPV)** is a red liquid given by mouth at two and four months with a third dose given at 6-18 months.

• **Measles, mumps and rubella (MMR)** is given once at 12-15 months.

• **Varicella (chickenpox)** is given once at 12-15 months.

• **Rotavirus (Rv)** is a new vaccine that prevents diarrheal diseases. It is given at two, four, and six months.

• A skin test for **tuberculosis** is usually given at 12-15 months, often at the same time the MMR is given.

Typical Immunization Schedule

At birth: Hepatitis B
1 week: Pneumoccal
2 months: HDTaP; hepatitis B; Rotavirus (Rv); polio
4 months: HDTaP; Rv; polio
6 months: HDTaP; hepatitis B; Rv; polio (can be
              later, up to 18 months)
12-15 months: MMR; Varicella; TB skin test

You don't like shots. Baby doesn't like shots. So, are all of these immunizations necessary? *Absolutely!*

Each of these diseases can cause death or very serious illness in children. *Don't take a chance with your baby!*

Keeping a record of *all* of your child's immunizations is essential. Keep it in your child's healthcare notebook. You'll need it when he goes to daycare or starts kindergarten. Some parents keep a copy of their child's immunization card in the diaper bag so it's always handy.

The public health department generally offers immunizations to babies at no charge. Sometimes the health department will provide immunizations at a local park or school. If you don't know where to take your baby for his shots, ask your school nurse for a recommendation.

Possible Reaction to Shots

When Nick got his shots, he got a lot of fever —
that really bothered him. He woke up at midnight with

a fever, and I gave him Tylenol. That helped.
Theresa, 16 - Nick, 6 months

Most babies have some reaction to immunizations.
Usually the reaction lasts only a day or two and is generally
mild. Giving your child a baby non-aspirin pain reliever
such as Tylenol or Pediacare will help relieve these
symptoms. See page 71 for suggestions about caring for a
feverish child.

Of course, if your baby has a severe reaction to his
immunizations (high fever for more than twelve hours or
other severe symptoms), you should call your doctor.

To repeat, *be sure* to keep a record of your baby's
immunizations. You will need these records to enroll your
child in school.

When Should You Call Your Doctor?

If your baby has a fever or seems sick, generally you
should call your healthcare provider. It's best to take baby's
temperature under his arm rather than sticking a thermometer into his rectum. A disposable or digital thermometer is
best for getting his underarm (called axillary) temperature.
These are available in drugstores. If you don't have one,
you can use a glass thermometer. If baby's temperature is
101° or higher, call your healthcare provider.

Also call his doctor if baby gets a sudden unexplained
rash.

If your baby spits up occasionally during her first two
months, it's probably nothing to worry about. This is
generally a combination of lumps of partially digested milk
combined with watery-looking fluid. They do this because
their digestive tract is not completely mature. This happens
more often with premature babies.

Give her small feedings often and handle her extra

gently after each feeding. She will probably spit up less often.

However, if baby, after every feeding, suddenly vomits most of his meal, call his healthcare provider immediately.

If you need to call your baby's healthcare provider, start by making some notes about your child's condition. Then you'll be able to describe his symptoms more accurately:

- Is he coughing? For how long?
- Has he lost his appetite?
- Does he have diarrhea?
- What is his temperature?
- Has he been exposed to any diseases? Has he received the immunizations he should have had by this time?

If your healthcare provider prescribes medication for your baby, be sure to ask if you should give baby all the medicine that's in the bottle. Or should you give it only for a certain number of days? Most antibiotics (Penicillin, Ampicillin, Ilison) need to be used until they are all gone. However, decongestants such as Pediacare and Dimetapp are to be used only when symptoms of congestion are present, i.e., when he has a stuffy, runny nose.

If Baby Has Diarrhea

Diarrhea can be a serious problem for a baby. This condition is not diagnosed simply by the baby having "too many" bowel movements a day. More important is the consistency of the BM.

If baby has a thin, watery, foul-smelling discharge, it's probably diarrhea. If she has this condition for as long as twelve hours, call your healthcare provider. A baby with diarrhea can quickly lose a dangerous amount of fluid.

You need to treat diarrhea by giving your baby clear liquids and nothing else for 24 hours. Liquids you should give him include Pedialyte (nonprescription liquid you buy in the drugstore or grocery store) or Pediapops, clear water, or water mixed with apple juice (one tablespoon apple juice to 8 ounces of water). Offer no solid foods, and feed him liquids as often as he'll take them.

Hernia? Check with Doctor

If you notice a bulge around your baby's navel or between his leg and tummy, check with your healthcare provider. He might have a hernia.

You're most likely to notice a bulge after baby has cried a lot or strained to have a bowel movement. Sometimes it will go away by itself, but occasionally it requires simple surgery. If your doctor recommends surgery, it's usually done during the second year of baby's life.

Dealing with Fever

If your child has a fever of 101° or higher, don't ignore it. Fever is one of the early signs of illness. If it's okay with your doctor, you can give baby Tylenol or other non-aspirin pain reliever.

You can sometimes bring a fever down by giving baby a cooling bath. If baby shivers while you're bathing him, it's too cold. A good way to do this is to put a towel in lukewarm water. Then wrap the baby in the wet towel. It helps bring his temperature down, and he's less likely to shiver.

Use lukewarm water, *not* alcohol. (A generation or two ago, people sometimes bathed a feverish baby in alcohol. This is a bad practice because the fumes can be dangerous for baby to breathe.)

Give your child extra liquids when he has a fever. If it's a sore throat that's causing his fever, your baby may not want to do a lot of sucking. A way to encourage your child to take lots of liquids is to give him popsicles (regular or

She doesn't feel so well today.

Pediapops). If a little piece breaks off in his mouth, it will
melt quickly and he can swallow it. This much sugar won't
hurt him.

Popsicles are also good for babies and toddlers if they
have a lot of nausea and vomiting. Sucking on a popsicle
will often help. You can freeze fruit juices to make your
own popsicles if you don't want to buy the sugary ones.
Besides being cold and making him feel better, homemade
juicesicles are nutritious.

Ear Infection? Call Doctor

> *Jonita had an ear infection which made her con-*
> *gestion problem even worse. Yes, I used to prop*
> *bottles. My mom probably still props them.*
>
> Ellen, 17 - Jonita, 6 months

If your child is uncomfortable and is pulling at his ears,
he may have an ear infection. Be sure to call your healthcare provider when this happens. A non-aspirin pain reliever can take away some of the pain and fever, but it does *not*
kill the germs causing the infection in his ear. An untreated

ear infection can result in hearing loss for your baby.

Ask your healthcare provider what to do if your baby gets an ear infection. She may want to see baby right away. Or she may recommend some things you can try first such as a decongestant. Do what she recommends, but don't ignore this illness.

To repeat, many infants' ear infections are caused by propped bottles. And that's one thing you can control!

Colds Are Common

Sujatha got a bad cold when she was four months old. She started coughing a lot, like she was choking. When she was breastfeeding, sometimes she would choke because the air couldn't come out of her runny nose. I took her to the doctor, but that didn't help. Finally my mom gave her some garlic tea, and she got over the cough and runny nose.

Kimiko, 17 - Sujatha, 5 months

Your baby will probably catch a few colds during his first two years. Colds are most contagious the first couple of days, This may be before the carrier knows he's sick, so it's impossible to protect your child completely from getting colds.

In *Nurturing Your Newborn,* you'll find Marlene's daily journal report of Evan's first cold when he was three weeks old. It was a miserable week for both Marlene and Evan.

No one, not even your doctor, can "cure" your child's cold. There is no known cure. Your job is to help baby feel as comfortable as possible. If he has a fever or headache, Tylenol may help.

If he has a runny or stuffy nose, use normal saline and a rubber syringe to clean the discharge from baby's nose. Normal saline is available from the drugstore without a prescription. The hospital probably gave you a rubber syringe for this purpose for baby.

Decongestant medicine may also make him feel better. If his nose is sore, cream or ointment on the area is soothing.

If he's coughing, your doctor may recommend cough medicine. If he has a stuffy nose, a cold-water vaporizer will help him breathe more easily. The old-fashioned steam vaporizers are dangerous, and they don't work as well.

If he doesn't want to eat, don't worry. When he's feeling better, he'll be hungry again. Encourage him to drink juice, water, clear soups, even a little weak tea.

How often your child has a cold depends on two things: the number of people with colds to whom he is exposed, and his own resistance.

If he's in good health generally, eats nutritious meals instead of junk foods, and gets plenty of rest, he is much less likely to get sick.

He May Have an Allergy

Makalah was sick off and on from when she was born. She just now got over a cold. It's mostly little colds or maybe allergies. She sneezes a lot, and her eyes get watery. She's very whiny when she's sick.
                                    Nykesha, 16 - Makalah, 9 months

Stuffy noses can be due to allergies. Allergies are caused generally by reactions to foods, plants, animals, or pollutants. A large percentage of allergies in children under two seem to be caused by food. Doctors generally recommend changes in diet for babies with these symptoms.

If a mother smokes during pregnancy, her baby is at greater risk for developing asthma and other allergies. When an infant or child breathes secondhand smoke, it can have the same effect. A smoke-free home is a wonderful gift to give your child. Not having to breathe smoke means he's less likely to get sick with a respiratory problem.

When I'm walking down the street and I smell
smoke, I know I wouldn't want my child smelling that.
Shaquala, 17- Haley, 9 months

If your baby has allergies, they might disappear in time as she becomes more adjusted to life on the outside. This is the reason most doctors don't start serious allergy testing until a child is much older, usually school age.

Caution — Sick Child

Makalah was especially fussy when she had pink
eye. The doctor told me to give her eye drops for five
days, even if her eyes cleared up earlier than that.
Nykesha

If your baby has something like conjunctivitis (pink eye) or impetigo (skin infection), you shouldn't have him around other children. You should take the same precautions during the first day or two he has a cold.

If you know a friend's child has one of these conditions, keep your baby away from him. Of course, later when your child is out in the neighborhood playing, he will pick up an illness occasionally because you can't control your neighbor's child. These generally aren't serious diseases. Mainly they're an annoyance to both you and your child that you avoid if you can.

One of the challenges of being a parent is keeping your child as healthy as possible. You need to do all you can to see that he has a good diet and gets plenty of sleep. See that he receives other good physical care — in addition to an unending supply of love.

If she's sick, check with your healthcare provider and follow his directions carefully. Do whatever you can to help your child be as comfortable as possible. Soon she will be her happy, active self again.

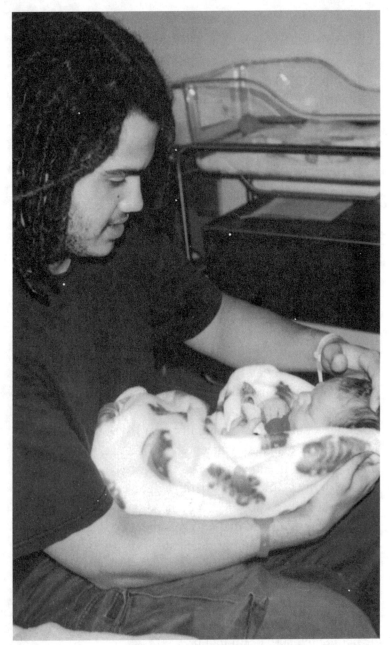

Dad is very special to him.

5

For Dad Only

I was scared when she told me she was pregnant. I was working, but I didn't know how I was going to support her and the baby. I couldn't even support myself. I was also real excited. I was happy but I was scared.

Katlia was scared, too. We were in this together.

I knew everything was going to be different. Nothing would ever be the same again. I felt like my freedom was going to be taken away. I couldn't come and go as I pleased, but I wanted to do the right thing. I wanted my daughter to have a father.

Raul, 19 - Elena, 23 months

*The first time I had to change him was an experi-
ence I won't forget. I had never changed a baby
before. It was weird because I never had to watch
over anyone, something so small that was mine.
Before I hadn't even worried about myself, and now I
have to give him a lot of my attention.*

Andy, 17 - Gus, 5 months (Yolanda, 15)

*We shared the night feedings. Luckily Dustin
started sleeping through the night real soon. We did it
all together. I don't think it would be fair if I just said
I'm not getting up, I'm not going to give him a bottle.
We shared the responsibility of having him. I think
you have to go 50-50.*

Mark, 22 - Dustin, 2½

Especially for Dads

Many teen mothers parent their child alone. This book is
written for them. It is *also* written for:

- Young couples who are parenting their child together.
- Young fathers who are involved with their child, or
  would like to be, whether or not they are still "with"
  their child's mother.
- Teen fathers who are parenting alone.

While most of these chapters are written to all teenage
parents, this chapter is especially for fathers. Chapter 6
focuses on the special needs of mothers parenting alone.

If you're a teen father (or an older father) and you're
reading this book, obviously you don't fit the stereotype of
the teen father who gets his girlfriend pregnant, then takes
no responsibility for his family. Whether you're married,
living with your baby's mother, or not living with her, you
probably are taking an important role in rearing your child.

Have you established paternity? If you and your child's

mother are not married, it's important that you legally establish paternity. If you don't, your child might not be able to claim Social Security, insurance benefits, veteran's and other types of benefits through you.

As you know, your child needs you. S/he needs your love and care and your financial support. Both you and your child's mother are required by law to support your child.

Sharing Care of Your Newborn

Mario feeds Carol, changes her, and plays with her. He even got up to feed her last night. He put her in her crib, and she started crying. So he picked her up and put her next to him, and she fell asleep. I'm glad she's like that. I'm glad she's attached to her dad.

Mario wanted to go fishing the other night. I said if it was cold, the baby and I would stay home. He went outside and decided it was warm enough, so we all went to the lake. He caught a fish and showed it to little Carol.

Let the baby get close to her father. It's really neat.

Kristyn, 17 - Carol, 3 months

Both you and your baby will "win" if you are deeply involved in child care. This can be a very special relationship for you two.

The play between a father and his baby tends to be quite active and generally includes a lot of talk. It can be especially exciting to the baby. Along with the activity, he enjoys the lower pitch of his father's voice. Even at a very early age, conversation between father and baby will occur quite easily. The father says words and baby responds with various sounds and facial expressions. In some families, babies look to mother for nurturing and comfort, and look forward to excitement and fun with dad. Both parents play a special role with their child.

Who Gets Up with Baby?

Night feedings? Diaper changings? I tried to help her, but I guess I really wasn't that great with me going to work. I was kind of a grouch getting up at 3 a.m. It was a lot of stress although Elena was a good baby. She got up more at night later.

The first month Elena would mostly sleep, but later when she got up she wouldn't want to go back to bed. It was hard for me to get back to sleep, too. I'd get up early and go to work, and I'd be exhausted. Gradually she started sleeping through the night.

On weekends I tried to spend as much time with Elena as I could, but I had to work a lot of overtime in order for us to manage. I remember working fourteen

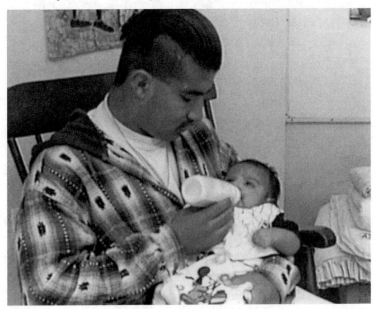

It's his turn to get up with baby tonight.

*hours a day, and it wasn't a choice. I had to. I
couldn't miss a day. Even when Elena was born at
5 a.m., after she was born, I went to work.*

Raul

If you are working and mom is home with the baby, you
may agree on a traditional separation of work with mom
taking care of the baby most of the time. Even then, having
a tiny baby in the house, one who is awake and crying
much of the night, makes it hard for mom to get enough
rest, and for you to get enough sleep to be alert at your job
the next day.

Many teenage parents, however, don't have the luxury of
one parent being home full-time with baby. Both mom and
dad may be in school, and both may also have a job. Ex-
pecting mom to care for the baby by herself is not very
rational. Caring for a baby takes a lot of energy. When
you share the work, you're more likely to share the joys
of parenting.

Rene and Greg weren't living together when Vanessa
was born. Greg was 19 and appeared pleased about the
pregnancy. He worked part-time the first year, and Rene
continued to live with her mother. Because he didn't live
with his child, he wasn't much involved in baby care.
When Vanessa was nine months old, Rene moved in with
Greg. Now they have a second baby, and Rene reports that
Greg is much more involved:

*During the week I get up with the baby because
Greg has to leave early in the morning, but on the
weekends he gets up at night. This was the deal we
made before Shavone was born.*

*We weren't living together when Vanessa was
born, and Greg kept complaining that he missed out
on a lot with her. We talked it over when I was*

pregnant again — about the things he would do and
what I would do. It's working pretty well.

If You Don't Live with Your Baby

Perhaps you and your child's mother have a close relationship but are not living together. Even if you don't live
with your baby's mother, you may be caring for your baby
as much as you can.

If you and baby's mother are not married, how much
"should" you be involved? If you live together, you probably feel much the same about joint parenting as do married
couples. If you don't live together, there is no pattern cut
and ready for you to follow. However, you can still play an
important role in your baby's life.

Shaun was away at college Monday through Thursday
each week during the first months after his baby's birth. He
spent weekends at his parents' home about three miles from
Beth Ann who lived with her parents. Troy didn't sleep a
lot during his first two months, and Beth Ann, 17, was
exhausted. Shaun decided he could help:

> *I'm very involved with Troy. I take him overnight*
> *once a week to give Beth Ann a break so she can*
> *catch up on her sleep. This way, I get to be with Troy.*
> *My mom or my sister help some, but I do most of it.*
> *For some reason, he has trouble sleeping at Beth*
> *Ann's house, but with me, he takes his bottle, eats,*
> *plays, and goes to bed. He sleeps five or six hours. I*
> *wish he'd do that for Beth Ann.*
>
> Shaun, 19 - Troy, 2 months

It's possible that Troy senses more stress at his mother's
house. It's also possible that having him only once a week
means Shaun has more energy to play with him. Babies

sense how a parent feels. If the parent is upset, baby probably is, too. If the parent relaxes, baby may do the same thing.

If you aren't with your baby's mother, you can still have a relationship with your child. Unless the court forbids it, you have a right to see your child and to spend time with her. Even if you aren't able to provide for her financially at this point, share your time.

Work out an arrangement so that your baby's mother also has some free time. Too often, the young mother is saddled with the entire responsibility of caring for the baby while the father doesn't even get to see his child. When this happens, everyone loses.

How Do Mom's Parents Feel?

When I see Alejandro, I have to take Anders over to his house because my mom doesn't want him over here. He comes and picks me up two or three times a week. When I'm over there, I have him do everything, except he hasn't given Anders a bath yet. He says he's scared Anders will slip. I figure when Anders is able to sit up, Alejandro won't be so scared.

Seilay, 16 - Anders, 3 weeks

Mother and baby may live with mother's parents. Her parents may have firm opinions about how much, if at all, the young father should be involved. This can be a difficult situation for everyone.

If Yolanda goes home and stays with her parents, I can't go over there and see my baby. When she's here, most of the time we take turns taking care of him. Yolanda isn't in school, so after school I go home and take care of him so she can sleep. Sometimes I have him on the weekends, sometimes she

does. We take turns going out — most of the time if we
stay at the house together, we end up fighting.

Andy

Yolanda and Andy are under a lot of stress. Her parents
still don't like Andy, and Yolanda is not happy living at
Andy's house. They need to talk about their feelings, work
through this stage, and know that they may feel less
stressed when Gus is a little older. It takes a lot of effort,
determination, and love to make a relationship work at any
age. It may be especially hard when the partners are
teenagers who already have a baby.

What About Marriage?

We waited for marriage because I wanted to make
sure it was right. I didn't want to end up with a

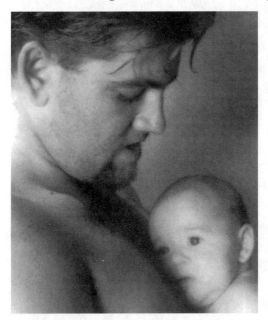

divorce when
he was 5 or so
and put him
through that
trauma. My
dad skipped
out on me,
and I didn't
want to put
my kid
through what
I went
through. We
didn't want to
rush into it.
Her parents
were real
stressed out,

He's developing a special relationship
with his dad.

and they were trying to plan a wedding for us, but no,
no, we didn't want to go.

Chris, 20 - Alex, 12 months

What about marriage? Should you marry *because* you're
having a child together? Getting married just because of the
pregnancy probably isn't a good idea. It's too easy for the
partners to blame each other when things get difficult later.
For this and other reasons, some couples choose to delay
marriage.

Chris and Erin were married when Alex was five months
old. Now Chris has a fairly good job and they have their
own little apartment, but it still isn't easy. Chris continued:

I have a lot of responsibility now. I feel a lot of
stress. I'm 20 years old and I feel like I'm 40. We go
shopping, and the baby gets this and Erin gets that,
and there may be $3 left for socks for me.

New Baby Hard on Relationships

I was never good with babies, but Keonia made me
understand babies' needs. Before she was born, my
husband and I were very close, but now we've drifted
apart. We seldom talk to each other anymore. We
argue more than usual.

Keonia makes me feel like I'm 30 years old. I feel
I'm not a little girl anymore or a carefree teenager. A
lot of times I feel that I'm giving all my love to my
daughter, and there isn't any left for my husband.

Lei, 16 - Keonia, 4 months

Many couples find that the stress of caring for a baby
combined with money problems is hard on their relationship. Lei and Roy were married a month before Keonia was
born. Keonia has had medical problems including two brief
stays in the hospital. Lei takes most of the responsibility for

her care while Roy leaves early in the morning for work and doesn't get back until after 6:00.

Hopefully Lei and Roy are able to talk about their relationship and make a conscious effort to regain their closeness. They may want to discuss their relationship with a counselor before they drift further apart.

Sometimes the father feels left out because mom appears to know more about caring for their baby than he does.

It's brought us together, but it's different because now Brooke feels it's more of a thing, "I'm the mother, I've been with him." It's more "I" than "We." That bothers me. It irks me to the point that I get downright mad.

Joel, 19 - Blair, 3 months

Probably the best thing for Joel to do is become an expert himself. He's far more than the baby-sitter, and he knows it. He and Brooke need to talk through these feelings. Probably Brooke will become a little less nervous, and, therefore, less bossy as Blair gets a little older. One thing is sure — nobody would win if Joel decided to quit caring for his son because he thinks the mother isn't as positive as he'd like.

Making Time for Partner

He's been saying I don't pay a lot of attention to him, I just focus on the baby. He says I don't care about him, I just care about the money. I tell him he's just too jealous, and that he should be proud of me for taking care of his daughter.

He says, "I'm a person, too." I tell him he's a full-grown man, and I remind him he can do all these things for himself, while Sujatha can't.

Kimiko, 17 - Sujatha, 5 months

He's listening while Dad whispers in his ear.

Sometimes a new father feels left out because his partner seems to give all of her time and attention to the baby. Mom can have some of those feelings, too:

> *He's very involved with her. In fact, he forgets all about me. He walks through the door and goes straight to her. I'll say, "Remember me?"*
> *He plays with her, feeds her, changes her diaper, everything. She looks like him.*
>
> Marsha, 16 - Justin, 5 months

You and your partner may find it's hard to make time for each other when you have a new baby. It's important for your baby's sake as well as your own that both of you continue to work toward a stronger and stronger relationship.

One of the reasons he fell in love with me is I talk
about our problems. I talk to him straight out — and
I'm here when he needs me. If he has a problem, I
support him. We both need to have a lot of patience.

Kimiko

Financial Problems May Occur

Financial problems tend to be intense for many teenage
couples. Even if dad has a job, the money probably won't
stretch as far as they'd like. Chris, like many young fathers,
works so hard supporting his family that he has little time
to spend with his son:

When Alex was born I was only making $6 an hour,
but I was determined this kid would be all right. I'd
get two jobs if I had to.

I didn't have a chance to discuss my feelings. I was
on my own from the time I was 16. I left home. I didn't
need anybody, and I was living pretty bad. I was
living on the streets.

I met Erin, and she kind of straightened me out. I
got a job, and tried to do something better with my
life. I think it might have helped to talk with other
young fathers, hear how they cope.

I don't get to see much of Alex. I leave here at 5:30
a.m., and get home at 7:30, so I see him for less than
an hour each evening. On the weekends we spend
time together.

School Is Important

If you're still in school, you probably can't support your
family by yourself. Most important for you right now is to
graduate and acquire job skills so you can become independent as soon as possible. Many young parents continue to
live with their parents until they're ready to be self-

supporting. Andy is struggling to finish school. Because there is no one else to care for their child, Yolanda is enrolled in independent study. Andy talked about their life together:

> *I want Gus to grow good. I don't want him to be in the streets or nothing. I'm going to try to teach him what's right and what's wrong. I don't want him to grow up like I did, or like my brothers.*
>
> *We have our difficult times. Yolanda gets those weird ideas when we don't have enough money, and we have to save for milk and diapers. Or when he's up crying at night, and I have to go to school. Most of the time when I'm up all night with Gus because he's sick, that's putting off my graduation.*
>
> *When I go to school Yolanda mostly stays with Gus during the day. Last week she got sick, too, and I had to take care of both of them. Last week I was at school only one day because both of them were sick.*
>
> *My mom and dad help me out a lot, but that's why I want to get out — so they won't have to worry about my baby.*
>
> *Other guys — I'd tell them to wait until they're through with school and have a job. It's hard with no money. It's hard trying to go to school with the baby whether you're a mother or a father.*

If you're already a father, you know that handling your responsibility is hard. Hopefully, you also know the *joys* that come along with those parenting responsibilities. Spend time with your child. You can be an extremely important part of his life.

For further information, see **Teen Dads: Rights, Responsibilities and Joys** *by Lindsay (Morning Glory).*

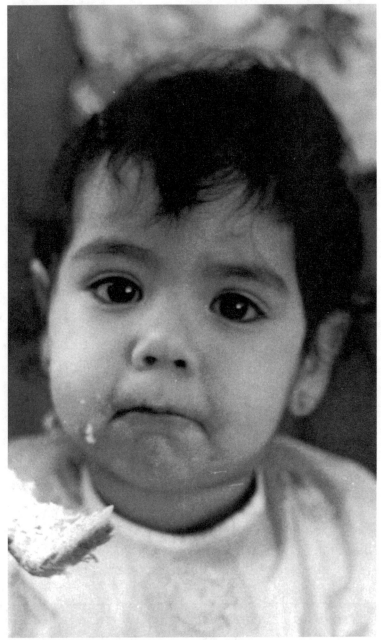

His mom is parenting alone.

6

If Mom
Is Alone

*I was fine all through my preg-
nancy except the last couple of
months were real hard on me. It
was stressful. I think it was
because I was worrying about a
lot of stuff.*

*Her father and I were together
off and on for a while, but we
didn't talk much. I would call him
to tell him how the baby was, and
he wouldn't call me. Was he going
to be in the baby's life? It's
stressful right now because he
says he wants to see the baby, but
he doesn't come over. I'm not
pressuring him to come see her.
He's almost 18, and he's in
school, too.*

I would like to be with him, but I don't think that it would work. He's the type of person who chooses his friends over other people. He goes out a lot with them, and he doesn't make time with the baby. Maybe later. His friends have been in a gang, and he hangs around with them.

Lacey, 16 - Jenilee, 1 month

No matter what, if you're pregnant, and you aren't with the baby's father, and your family doesn't support you, your baby will need you 24 hours a day.

Kimiko, 17 - Sujatha, 5 months

About five out of six teenage mothers are not married when they give birth. Some of these young mothers are quite alone. The baby's father may have left when he learned of the pregnancy. In some cases, he may not even know about the baby.

On Being Positive — and Honest

Haley's father is not around, and I'm engaged to somebody else. My fiancé is in the army right now, but he acts like her father. I'll tell her who her father is. He's a drug addict and hasn't seen her. I can't trust him when he calls and wants to take her out.

Shuquala, 17 - Haley, 9 months

Do I Have a Daddy? by Lindsay (2000: Morning Glory Press) is a picture book for the child who doesn't know his biological father. Included in the book is a section of suggestions for a single mother. Young mothers share their thoughts on this important topic. These young mothers stress two things:

• Be honest with your child.
• Be as positive as possible.

For some young mothers, these goals are in conflict. Perhaps at this point you find it hard to say anything good about your child's father. Raylene is in this position:

> *I thought maybe because Rick is Victor's dad, I should give marriage a thought. But I knew I would be getting into the same abuse my mom is in except Rick didn't drink.*
>
> *He was mean when he was sober, while my dad does it when he's drunk. I didn't even consider marrying him.*
>
> *Rick would say, "You'll never find anybody else. Guys will think you're a whore." The last time he hit me was six weeks before Victor was born. I realized I deserved better. I would rather be alone and single forever than put up with that.*
>
> Raylene 18 - Victor, 2

Talking in a positive way with Victor about his father will be hard for Raylene. However, in *Do I Have a Daddy?* Robin says:

> *Why make a kid feel like his father was a louse? If his dad's a louse, that makes him half-louse. It's not fair to lay your feelings on your child.*
>
> *I tell Stu, "Your father wasn't as lucky as I am — he didn't get to live with you.*
>
> Robin, 21 - Stu, 5

Robin is right. It's important for your child's sake that you try to look beyond your own feelings. This will be difficult for Raylene. She may decide to level with Victor at some time, and tell him that she and his father had a very poor relationship. With the passage of time, perhaps she will also be able to share some positive memories with her son.

Filing for Child Support

Your child is more likely to be poor if he has only one
parent supporting him. Both you and your child's father are
required by law to support your child. It doesn't matter
whether or not you planned to have a child together.

Your child has a right to benefits from both of you.
These include Social Security, insurance benefits, inherit-
ance rights, and veteran's benefits. Your child will be able
to claim such benefits if paternity has been established. In
some states, paternity is established by both mother and
father signing a legal paper saying he is the father.

Is your child's father insisting he is not the father? If so,
you may need to go to court. Blood tests are almost 100
percent accurate in identifying the father of a child. The
blood tests are genetic tests which compare many different
factors in your blood with similar parts of the man's and
the child's blood.

Some couples are close throughout much of the
pregnancy, then split up before the baby is born. Kellie's
situation is typical:

> *We aren't together now but Ron's paying child
> support. He hasn't seen Kevin since he was a
> month old.*
>
> *We had been together for two years, and we were
> close up to my eighth month. He was excited about the
> whole thing. Then Ron's parents separated, and his
> brother was getting divorced. He got scared that
> would happen to us.*
>
> *Ron was back with me for about a month after
> Kevin was born, then left again. Now he's trying to
> come back. I'm not going to let that happen because I
> don't want Kevin hurt again, and I don't want to
> be hurt.*

Your child has a right to benefits from both parents.

We had talked of marriage. Then in just one week we went from planning marriage to he never wanted to see me again. I think he's scared of growing up and taking responsibility.

I wouldn't think it was possible, but Ron's feelings seemed to change overnight. I think it had a lot to do with his mother. Once I got pregnant, she went totally against me. I was fine, good enough for him until I got pregnant. Then she decided I was trying to trap him. We had a good relationship those two years. We hardly ever fought.

Kellie, 16 - Kevin, 3 months

It's impossible to say what Kellie "should" do. Perhaps she and Ron will eventually decide to parent together — or they may not. In either case, Kellie is wise to have filed for child support. She also may decide, even if she and Ron are not together, that Ron and Kevin need to have a relationship.

Some young mothers insist they will not file for child support. "We don't need him," they say. Sometimes they don't even name the father of their baby.

It's the child who loses out when this happens. Maybe your baby's father has no job and no money now. Perhaps you don't think you want your child to know him. It's still important that you don't shut him out of your child's life forever.

"I Still Like Him"

Beth has very mixed feelings about her child's father:

> *At first Al saw the baby about every other day, or called up to see how she was. Then I decided I didn't want him to see Patty any more. I told him, and we*

A single parent can certainly be a loving, "good" parent.

*argued about it. He has the right, I know, and he
really does care about her. I had thought he was the
type of guy who would say, "So I have a baby, so
what?" but he's not.*

*Al had planned to coach me during labor, then we
started arguing. The subject wasn't brought up again.
I found another coach, a friend of mine.*

*I haven't seen Al much for quite awhile. When I
was first pregnant, we were going to get married. But
I didn't want to get married just because of the
pregnancy — I think that's a big mistake. Maybe
when he works out what he wants to do with his life...*

*Perhaps the real reason I don't want him to see
Patty is because I still like him. When he's around
here I get really upset. So maybe if/when I don't have
these feelings, it will be the right time for him to
come around.*

*Now I still care for him a lot, and when I see him
with his daughter, I feel sad. I wish things could have
worked out. I know he has the right to see her, but I'm
not ready for it, that's all.*

Beth, 18 - Patty, 3 weeks

If the baby's father is providing some financial support,
and sometimes even if he's not, he has a right to see his
baby. Legally, he may be able to have his child with him
part of the time.

If the young parents disagree on this matter, they should
talk to a lawyer or legal aid group.

Dad May Be Far Away

Sometimes the baby's father can't be with his family. He
may be in the armed forces, or he may be away for other
reasons:

*Jayme has seen his dad once. I took him to the
prison when he was 6 months old. I felt very
uncomfortable with Cory, and so did Jayme.*

*It was difficult for me because Cory looked differ-
ent, his attitude was different, and I was different. I
didn't feel as though we had conceived this child
together.*

Kaylene, 18 – Jayme, 16 months

What is Kaylene's responsibility to Jayme and to his
father? Should she try to maintain a relationship with Cory
for Jayme's sake? If Cory is to have a relationship with
Jayme, Kaylene can help by sending lots of photos to him,
and keeping him up to date on his son's development.

Handling Future Relationships

*I've been alone since I was three weeks pregnant,
but I've been seeing somebody else for about two
months. Jayme loves my new friend. He's starting to
notice people are around a lot more, and he gets real
attached to people fast. He's used to just me being
around, but he's definitely getting into Mommy being
with someone else. He likes being a family.*

*I hadn't dated much before that. I had dated once,
but that didn't work out because the man I was seeing
didn't like kids. He didn't want to be a daddy or
anything close, so I ended that real fast.*

Kaylene

Young mothers who are alone may wonder how to
handle future relationships. How soon should you tell a
new friend about your child? Most moms agree that it's
important to be honest.

"If he doesn't want to have anything to do with me
because I have a baby, he's not for me," they say. On the

other hand, sometimes a new boyfriend seems too eager to be a father to the child:

> *Dating other people is hard. I dated one person who liked me, but he thought the only reason I wanted to go out with him was for him to be a father to Kevin. Another one was already putting money away for his college.*
>
> *Finding the right person is going to be hard. It's going to have its ups and downs. I want to find somebody who's not afraid, but who doesn't want to take over the whole situation.*
>
> Kellie

Finding the "right" approach to future relationships can be difficult. You might like your child to have an acting father. At the same time you don't want her to assume that every man who comes around is going to be her dad. When you have a child, handling dating and your relationship with a possible future partner takes a great deal of wisdom, love, and caring.

Single Parenting Can Work

About half the children in the United States today will spend at least part of their lives in a one-parent household. Most people still think it's better for a child to have two parents who care about each other. But a single parent can certainly be a loving, "good" parent. It just takes a little more effort.

Time with Grandma is very special.

7

Three-Generation Living

- **Help from Grandma**
- **"Who's My Mother?"**
- **Role of Brothers and Sisters**
- **Key — Taking Responsibility**
- **Moving in with Partner's Family**

I could baby-sit easily, but when it came to my baby, I needed my mom. She was too bossy, but I did need her. I wish she could have sometimes asked me instead of telling me what to do.

Mom thinks her way is much better because she's older. But I'm a mother, too, and I think I could baby-sit easily, but when it came to my baby, I needed my mom. She was too bossy, but I did need her. I wish she could have sometimes asked me instead of telling me what to do.

Mom thinks her way is much better because she's older. But I'm a mother, too, and I think I should try my way to see if it works.

If I were living on my own, I think I'd be a nervous wreck. I wouldn't have anyone to ask for advice. But there are times when I want to try something myself because I want to be the responsible person.

Holly, 17 - Orlando, 5 months

Living with my family is good because I get a lot of help. But at times it's like, "Oh, you should do this." Of course I listen because my mom's not going to tell me anything bad.

Seilay, 16 - Anders, 3 weeks

When we fight, there are always people around. My mom takes his side always — and when we lived at his house, his mom and dad were always on my side!

Ynez, 16 - Lenny, 3 months

Help from Grandma

When I came home from the hospital, sometimes I'd feel scared. I didn't know what to do. I was even scared to carry Racquelle. When she cried and cried, I cried myself because I didn't know what was wrong.

Cheryl, 15 - Racquelle, 2 months

Teenage parents, married as well as single, are more likely to live with their parents than is an older family. How does this change their approach to baby care and child rearing?

On the positive side, it is often reassuring as well as less tiring to have some help with baby care. New parents may suddenly feel they don't know how to take care of this small creature. Having your mother in the same house can be reassuring. During the early weeks of night feeding, she may even be willing to take an occasional turn at getting up with the baby while you sleep.

*She loves me and she loves the baby, but the baby
is my responsibility. A couple of times Sonja would
wake up at night and cry and cry. I would cry, too,
and Mom would come in and help. But I want Sonja to
know me as her mother.*

Julie, 16 - Sonja, 7 months

If baby's father isn't around, you may need more help
from grandma. Many young mothers who live with their
parents find the first couple of months with a baby somewhat of a "honeymoon" period. Your parents may be eager
to help you.

If you have brothers and sisters, they may fight over who
gets to hold the baby next. Appreciate their help even as
you do as much as possible for your baby.

"Who's My Mother?"

The neat thing about grandmas is that they're experienced. They've learned from their mistakes. They take
time, and have learned how to be patient with a fussy baby.

The not-so-good news is that sometimes grandparents
take on too much responsibility. They may appear to forget
who the mom is.

If grandmother takes over in the beginning, it may be
hard for baby's own mother to take charge later. The result
in many families is a baby who thinks grandma is her
mother. Baby's mother then feels left out and resentful.
Most hurt may be baby who isn't sure who mother really is.

*I catch my mother occasionally playing the mother
role. I can understand that because she has the
experience. Besides, I really need that when I'm tired
or don't feel good. But other times I don't like it. I'll
be playing with Karl, and she'll come in and pick him*

up and take him off with her. I don't like that at all.

I take Karl with me everywhere I can, and my mother is constantly telling me I shouldn't do that, that I'm not being fair to Karl. But if I had to stay home all the time with him, I'd be miserable. And if I'm miserable, so is Karl. I think it's all right. He's seeing new things, being with people. He's learning more from going places with me.

Sometimes I have to explain to my mom that I have taken on this responsibility of being a mother, and I want to do it the whole way. I know when Karl is hungry, when he needs a bath, etc., but my mom still tries to tell me to do all these things. I try not to let it bother me — but it does.

Because I'm underage, it would be hard to live alone. I wouldn't have anybody around when I'm sick. I wouldn't have anybody to talk to — and I couldn't afford a place of my own.

Kimberly, 17 - Karl, 2 months

Role of Brothers and Sisters

If you have brothers and/or sisters living with you, you'll need to consider their feelings, too. Will their lives change much because of your baby? Will they be expected to do more of the housework because you'll be so busy with your child?

How do you think they will feel about that? There probably is no "right" answer, but it's a topic you and your family should consider, preferably before baby arrives.

Sometimes my sisters want to give me advice. I let them say what they want. I can ignore them.

For example, just lately Stevie gets crabby when he's having a bowel movement. When they see him

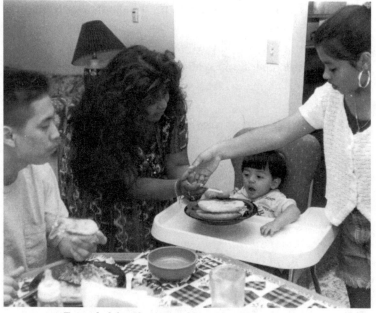

Extended family — more commotion, more love.

*fussing, they tell me to feed him. Or they think we
should "do" something. They'll shake toys in front of
his face. But he's too little to care much about toys.*

*When he was just two weeks old, they wanted to
shake rattles in his face. He didn't want that. He's just
a little baby. I'd tell them that, and they'd go running
to tell my mom, "Alison doesn't want us to do anything with her baby." My mom would laugh and tell
them I know what I'm doing.*

*I think my sisters get annoyed at my being here all
the time with the baby. But when I ask them to baby-
sit so I can go out for a little while, they usually
refuse.*

Alison, 18 - Stevie 2 months

Alison's sisters are in their early teens. They don't
understand that Alison needs to be away from Stevie once

in awhile. Perhaps Alison could try a little harder to include her sisters in caring for Stevie when they want to be included. Perhaps then they would be more willing to take care of him occasionally when Alison needs to leave for a short time.

Key — Taking Responsibility

I thought it would be my mom taking care of Racquelle all the time. With my two sisters who got pregnant at 16, she took over. They didn't know anything about taking care of their babies.

When I brought Racquelle home, I took care of her all the time. I showed my mom I could do it. So now that she knows she doesn't have to take care of her, she will baby-sit sometimes when I want to go out.

Cheryl

Sometimes young mothers have more help than they want. If this happens to you, perhaps you can help your family understand that all of you — your parents, siblings, baby, and you — will be better off if you take the primary responsibility for caring for your child. If you start out, tired as you are, showing them that you know how to be a good parent, they may be less likely to give you more help and advice than you feel you need. Alison's mother said:

Alison does everything. If I weren't working, it would be harder not to take over. I'm surprised at myself that I haven't done that. That was a concern I had when she was pregnant. I knew this had to be her baby, her responsibility. I love babies, and I like to take care of them, but I've not gotten up even once with Stevie. In fact, I don't hear him cry at night!

Alison added:

Stevie's such a good baby, but I do think I have to keep him quiet. Dad can take quite a bit, but I know he doesn't like to hear babies cry. It would be a lot harder if he were a fussy baby. Then I think my family might get irritated. But since he sleeps in my room, I just pick him up and nurse him when he wakes up at night. He goes right back to sleep.

If you're a young parent living with your parents, you may feel you have no choice. You probably also appreciate their help. An extended family of baby, mother, and/or father, and grandparents at its best means more love and TLC (Tender Loving Care) for baby — and that's great! Sometimes the relationship between a teen mom and her mother even improves after the baby is born:

My relationship with my mom became a little better because I started thinking about my kids and how I wanted my kids to treat me. And I started thinking of her as a friend as well as a mother. She really really respects me in my motherhood. She doesn't act like I'm just a little kid trying to raise a baby.

Kellie, 16 - Kevin, 3 months

Moving in with Partner's Family

If you move in with your partner's family (whether you're the mother or father), there may be added difficulties. No two families are alike, and those differences may demand a lot of understanding on everybody's part. Zandra talked about living with Nathan's family while she was pregnant, then moving with Nathan and their baby to her mother's home in another state. It's a difficult situation:

Before, I lived with Nathan's family when I was pregnant. Nathan was going to school, he was

*working . . . I would just stay in the room all day when
I was there. I didn't like being around them when he
was at work or at school. If Nathan wasn't there, I
wouldn't eat with his family. I would take my food to
my room.*

*But now we live here and they're 1500 miles away.
And now it's hard for Nathan because he hates my
family. He's a good person, he's nurturing to Dakota,
but he's not happy here.*

Zandra, 16 - Dakota, 11 months

Camelia worried about moving in with Jonah's family:

*When I first moved in, I thought everyone was
against me. I thought, they're family, and they'll stick
up for each other, but I was wrong.*

*I love my mother-in-law. She's like my second
mom. Considering that I was pregnant, I was going
through a lot of mood swings.*

*The one thing I was mostly mad about was I didn't
have my mom here to go to. It was funny for me to
think that way because I was the one who decided
to move out.*

Camelia, 16 - Buchanan, 6 months

Life is seldom easy when two families live together. If
you're a guest of your partner's family, you'll want to do
all you can to foster positive relationships. Your first task is
to communicate with your partner.

Communication doesn't mean you tell him (or her) how
bad his parents are. Rather, it's a matter of the two of you
working together to work through the problems. Whether
you're dealing with big issues or little day-to-day annoy-
ances, do all you can to find solutions so everyone wins.

Part III
Your Baby Is
Ready to Move

During the middle four months of your child's first year, she will change from a lie-where-you-put-her baby to a little person on the move. She may not be standing or crawling by her eighth-month birthday, but she's getting close. Her development during this time is described in the next chapter.

Keeping baby safe will become a greater challenge as he starts crawling. Childproofing is discussed in chapter 9.

Baby's eating habits change, too, from four to six months of breast- or bottle-feeding only to small beginnings in the solid food arena. Chapter 10 is about that first move toward the kinds of food you eat, that short period of time when your baby is ready for solids but can't yet manage lumps in his food. It's a time when you'll still do most of the feeding, although baby will eat some foods with his fingers.

Playing with baby becomes more and more fun for him and for you. Perhaps in chapter 11 you'll find some new ideas for playing with and teaching your child.

Her curiosity makes her want to touch and handle everything.

8

Baby Is Much More Active

Now, at five months, Orlando is more alert, more a person. When he was little, he just lay there and really couldn't see me clearly. Now he rolls over, coos, growls (really!), plays with his feet and his hands, and laughs.

When he was a newborn, I held him a lot, and he loved that. Now, I hold him and play with him. I spend about as much time playing with him now as I did holding him, perhaps a little more. He's teething, and is a little fussy.

Holly, 17 - Orlando, 5 months

Nick sits up by himself for a long time, then he collapses. Then I set

*him up again. When he gets tired, he lies down. He
entertains himself for a longer time now.*

Theresa, 16 - Nick, 6 months

His Interests Grow

*Delphina has a mobile of bears with music, and she
grabs them. She loves sitting in a swing and watching
the mobile go around.*

Shoshana, 17 - Delphina, 4 months

By four months, your baby's curiosity is growing fast,
and he wants to touch and handle everything possible. A
simple face drawn on a paper plate and taped to his crib
interests a newborn. No longer, however, can you give him
such a flimsy thing to look at.

He will enjoy a well-designed mobile, but now his
mobile must be strong enough to be hit, pulled, and abused
— if he can reach it at all. It's less frustrating to baby to
have the mobile placed close enough to be touched and
handled.

At this age, he needs a crib toy. It must be "battable" and
safe. It also should make a noise, such as several rattles
hanging within batting range. Using string around baby is
risky in case he could wrap it around his neck. An inexpensive cradle gym is a good purchase. It should have simple
objects that baby can hit, pull, and handle.

Sometime during this stage, baby will be able to reach
for things he sees. This is quite different from his earlier
batting at objects. Now he sees the object, reaches for it
smoothly, and opens his fingers before he touches it. What
a change!

He's Moving Around

*Juan pulls on the handle of the cradle gym in the
playpen. He pulls it down, then lets it go. He got*

frustrated this morning because he tried to crawl to
get what he wanted, and he just couldn't do it.

Ginny

Four-month-old Sara stays pretty much where you put
her. Lay her on a blanket with a few toys. Go back ten
minutes later, and she's in the same general area. She may
be able to dig her toes in and scoot a little. Soon she will
turn from her back to her stomach and back again, but she's
not moving all over the apartment yet.

Eight-month-old Sam is an entirely different being. He's
sitting up. He's getting ready to crawl. In fact, lay him on a
blanket on the floor, turn your back for a second, and he
may be across the room! He may be crawling already.

The physical changes happening between four and eight
months in a baby's life are startling. Until he's four or five
months old, baby is limited to lying on his back or his
stomach, or being propped up by someone else. He depends
completely on others to move him from place to place.

By about 61/2 months, many babies sit up by themselves.
Many start creeping or crawling about a month later. But,
as in every kind of development, each child is different.
Don't worry if your baby isn't sitting up or crawling yet.

Wayne's been crawling since seven months, but he
didn't sit up until about that time. I like the crawling
because now he can do something.

Lorice Ann, 23 - Wayne, 9 months; Kelton, 7 years

Sometime toward the end of this four-to-eight-month
period, your baby may pull herself to a standing position.
She'll hang on for dear life to her crib railing or to the arm
of the couch. At first she's pleased, but in a minute she may
start crying. She doesn't know how to sit down again!

You can help her learn to sit down. Show her how.

Gently bend her knees as you talk to her. She'll sit down, and two minutes later she's up again. It may take several days for her to learn to get down by herself.

Comparing Babies

The age at which a baby sits up, crawls, and walks seems to have nothing to do with her I.Q. when she's older. Comparing your child's development to that of your friend's child can be fun as long as you don't take these differences in development as negative for either child. The baby who doesn't move off the blanket during much of her first year may be one of the brightest kids around.

To some parents, baby's intellectual development is very important. There are many kinds of intelligence. One child may be very interested in learning pre-reading skills; another may be fascinated with insects, and spend lots of time watching them move. Perhaps your child can hardly wait for an opportunity to help mom or dad fix things around the house.

The child who doesn't read well in kindergarten may be repairing the family car a few years later, a task her reading brother may find impossible.

Remember that your child, whatever his abilities, is important; your child is a fun person. Enjoy him. Whether or not he is "brilliant" is not terribly important.

Curiosity Leads to Crawling

These past couple of weeks Jonita has started pulling herself up on the chair. She likes to stand, and doesn't like to sit very often. This morning my sister got her up and set her in the living room. She went in the bedroom, and when she came out, Jonita was clear across the room!

Ellen, 17 - Jonita, 6 months

As baby lies on the floor or sits in his infant seat, his curiosity is building rapidly. Put yourself in his place. Imagine what it must be like not to be able to move. You see all those exciting things around you, and all you can do is look at them. Imagine the frustration!

> *She's crawling now. Before, she got mad because*
> *she couldn't reach stuff. Now she gets into things.*
> *She's cruising around the living room now.*
>
> Shaquala, 17 - Haley, 9 months

Wanting to satisfy his curiosity is baby's biggest reason for learning to crawl. He likes the exercise and being able to move his body, but satisfying his curiosity is the big incentive.

Before they walk, babies get around in a variety of ways. Classic crawling is getting up on his hands and knees and moving around. Some babies pull themselves along on their tummies. Others stand up on their feet and hands, then

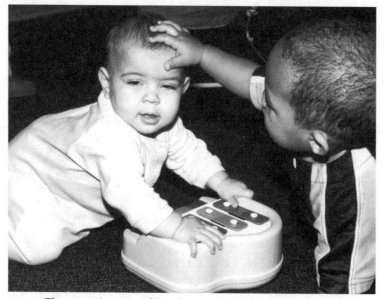

They examine everything they can reach, even each other.

"walk" like a little puppy. Whichever method your baby chooses, he is delighted that he can finally get around.

Did you know that baby needs your help to learn to crawl? No, you don't need to show her how to move her legs and arms. It is important, though, that you give her lots of opportunity to move around. That means not caging her in a playpen or setting her in her high chair for long periods of time.

Instead, put her on the floor on a blanket. Dress her so she won't hurt her knees, and let her go. And before you know it, she will go — all over the house! Of course, you need to baby-proof your home by this time.

> *When Lynn started crawling, I couldn't sit around any longer and not watch her when she was on the floor. She's going all the time — and so am I!*
>
> Sheryl Ann, 17 - Lynn, 7 months

> *Clark didn't crawl two weeks ago, but now he speeds all over the place. What a change!*
>
> Kathleen, 18 - Clark, 7 months, and Aaron, 2 years

Build Trust by Responding

> *Jay is a good baby. He only cries when he wants something, has messy pants, or wants to eat. He does have his fussy days when he just wants to cry. Yesterday was one of those.*
>
> *I barely got home from school when he started crying, and he didn't stop until 10 p.m. when he went to bed. I think he's cutting teeth. Sometimes it's hard having a baby.*
>
> Bev, 17 - Jay, 8 months

It's still important to respond to your baby's cries as promptly as possible. Letting him learn he can trust you to take care of his needs is not going to spoil him. Unhappy, dissatisfied, "spoiled" babies are far more likely to be

babies who are already learning they can't depend on
mother to come when they need her.

> *I've heard so many times that I'm spoiling*
> *Buchanan. I can't stand it when people tell me how to*
> *raise my son. I don't believe in spoiling him. I just*
> *want him to be secure, to know I'll be there for him. If*
> *he's crying, he's crying because he needs something. I*
> *want him to know that if he cries, I'll be there.*
>
> Camelia, 16 - Buchanan, 6 months

Continue to hold your baby, and to rock him. Now you'll
be able to do a lot more with him. This stage is usually
delightful for parents.

Some babies have a hard time settling down to sleep.
They may fuss for a time before going to sleep, and that's
okay. If the fussing changes to a hard cry, of course it's
time to do something.

Throughout most of this period, baby may be happy
most of the time, just as he was in the less active one-to-
four-month stage. He giggles and laughs, mimics what
you're doing, and generally has a wonderful time throughout much of his day. But he wants you to be nearby. If
mother leaves for more than a few hours, the separation
may be hard on both her and her child:

> *I went to the mountains for three days without*
> *Lynn, and it was hard. I couldn't really have fun*
> *because I was always thinking about her, and won-*
> *dering if she was all right. I knew she was being taken*
> *care of okay, but it still bothered me. When I got back,*
> *she wouldn't let me out of her sight.*
>
> Sheryl Ann

This doesn't mean it's wrong to take some time for
yourself. It does mean you will choose carefully the person

She loves to play on the floor with Mom.

who will care for your child while you're gone. You also
need to be prepared for a short period of increased
dependence on you when you return.

Baby's Fears

*Haley is afraid of heights. She'll look down from
her bed and get scared. I hold her and cuddle her.*

Shaquala

Some babies develop rather strong fears. Sometimes it's
the vacuum cleaner. It might be the lawn mower or some
other loud noise. He may decide he wants nothing to do
with new places or different situations. A trip to the store
may upset him.

If it's the vacuum cleaner, you could try using it while he
sleeps. A better way is to let him look and explore the
vacuum cleaner before you turn it on. Then hold him with

one arm (lovingly, not scoldingly) while you clean for a few minutes. Don't overdo it, of course, but he may accept the noise under these conditions.

Always, whatever his age, treat your child's fears as the realities they are. It absolutely does not matter that you know "there is nothing to be afraid of." The fact is that he is afraid. You need to help him deal with his fear, not scold him.

Time for Teeth

When Dale was teething, I didn't even know he was. He would be cranky once in awhile, but I just thought he was tired or something.

Arlene, 17 - Dale, 11 months

The "average" baby (yours may be quite different) cuts her first teeth when she is six or seven months old. She will probably get her lower incisors first. By eight or nine months, she may have four of her upper teeth.

Some babies fuss when their teeth are cutting through their gums. Others seem to notice very little, if any, discomfort. One mother reported she knew her child had cut his teeth when she heard the spoon clanking against the tooth.

Sujatha is teething now, and I don't know what to do. We do everything we can, and she still cries — except when I put my finger in her mouth and rub her gums.

Kimiko, 17 - Sujatha, 5 months

For some babies, teething is a painful experience. She may want to bite everything in sight. Give her a teething ring. Store several in the freezer. If the ring is cold, she'll like it better.

*Robin has a tooth that's not all the way in. She's
keeping me up for hours. Nothing seems to work.
I put teething lotion on it, or ice cubes, but
nothing helps.*

Melinda, 15 - Robin, 9 months

Try freezing thin slices of cantaloupe for your teething
baby. Of course you carefully remove all seeds and rind
from the melon. Baby can suck on the frozen piece and,
when it thaws, gum it and swallow it.

You can buy teething lotion which may help soothe
painful gums. Put it on baby's gums a few minutes before
feeding time. It may take away some of the pain so that she
can eat more comfortably.

*I got a pain reliever for teething, and that helps. I
also got those toys for her to bite on.*

Shaquala, 17 - Haley, 9 months

*The teething was really hard because Shareef got
the four top ones all at once. I put teething rings in
the freezer, and gave them to her when they were real
cold. She loves the new vibrating things that you bite
and it vibrates. The cold ring or a cold rag also
helped a lot.*

Adia, 17 - Shareef, 11 months

Baby may drool while she's teething. If so, tie a
terrycloth bib on her.

These first teeth are not chewing teeth. They won't help
much when she's trying to chew food. She'll still have to
gum solid food with lumps in it. But she may try to chew
the nipple on her bottle.

If you're breastfeeding, she may try biting your nipple. If
the nipple is well back in her mouth, as it should be for
sucking, she can't bite. The only problem is when she stops

sucking and decides to play.

If she bites, remove your nipple from her mouth with a firm "No." Pause for a few seconds even if she's whimpering because you've taken her food away. Then if she wants to eat, let her. But don't let her bite you. Many breastfed babies learn not to bite after only a day or two of this approach.

If your baby gets a fever, don't blame it on teething. She may fuss, she may even have a tiny bit of fever if her teeth are bothering her. But if she has a "real" fever (higher than 101^0), she's sick. A fever indicates an infection. Call your healthcare provider.

At six months, she's happy much of the time.

Guard against cavities in those little teeth from the beginning. Encourage her to drink water. It's certainly better for her teeth than are sweet drinks, and water helps rinse milk and other foods out of her mouth.

Avoid sweet foods. During this period you should be able to keep candy and other sweets almost entirely away from baby. If she doesn't know about them, she won't cry for junk foods. The same suggestion applies to soda and other soft drinks. Don't even give her a taste. Her teeth will thank you.

Nursing Bottle Syndrome

Even a bottle of formula can be a problem for baby's teeth. True, her teeth need a lot of calcium in order to develop properly and to stay healthy. The best source of calcium is formula (or breastmilk). She needs about 20 ounces of formula each day at this stage.

A bottle of formula is a problem if she keeps the bottle nipple in her mouth as she falls asleep, and it stays there. Formula dribbling into her mouth during the night keeps her teeth covered with a film of milk. Formula, nutritious as it is, has enough natural sugar in it to damage teeth if it stays there hour after hour.

Dentists see so many toddlers with rotten little teeth in front that they have given this condition a name: Nursing Bottle Syndrome.

The solution, if baby wants a bottle in bed with her, is to fill the bottle with water. Fruit juice is even worse than formula because it has more sugar in it. If she needs the sucking when she goes to sleep, she can get it with a bottle filled with water or with a pacifier.

Taking a bottle of formula to bed can become a very strong habit, a habit that is hard to change. If you hold her while she drinks her bottle at bedtime, she won't need more formula in bed. When she's big enough to take the bottle to bed with her, always put water in it. Then she won't risk having Nursing Bottle Syndrome.

Tremendous Changes Already!

Your pre-toddler has changed tremendously in these first eight months. As she sits up, possibly stands, maybe scoots across the floor, you may think she's into everything already. But amazingly soon she will be walking, then running. Keeping up with her will be — already is — an exciting challenge. *Are you ready?*

Protective covers on the electrical outlets help keep her safe.

9

Accident-Proofing Your Home

I keep a lock on the door under the sink so Gary can't get into it.

Jan, 15 - Gary, 12 months

My mother always said not to put my soaps and things in a low cupboard, so I keep them up high above the stove.

Olivia, 20 - Henry, 11 months

Leon pushes a chair up to the counter and gets up in the top cupboard looking for little goodies. I have glasses up there, so I suppose I'll have to fasten the doors shut. I keep him locked out of the bathroom.

Tamera, 21 - Leon, 10 months;
DeeDee, 4 years

Accidents — Often Deadly

Accident-proofing your home is *absolutely* essential if you have a baby, toddler, or preschooler living there. Accidents injure and kill many young children every year. In fact, accidents are by far the greatest cause of injury and death for this age group — thousands are permanently crippled or killed annually. Keeping your child safe is one of your biggest challenges.

The chief causes of fatal accidents for children under one year are suffocating and choking. Cars, fires, drowning, and poisoning cause the most fatal accidents for toddlers and preschoolers. Falls cause about forty percent of all injuries to young children.

Warning
Never leave baby alone on a changing table, bed, or other off-the-floor surface for a second. The baby who couldn't turn over yesterday may do so today.

When you visit friends, put your tiny baby's blanket on the floor. She can nap there as well as she could on the bed, and she'll be much safer. She can't fall off the floor. Be sure she's protected from house pets and small children.

Your baby should not have a pillow in her bed. A pillow could cause a breathing problem if she got her face buried in it. If grandma made a beautifully embroidered pillow for her, appreciate it, but keep it out of her crib.

Until she can turn over by herself, always lay baby on her back to sleep. This lessens the danger of SIDS (Sudden Infant Death Syndrome).

A propped bottle is dangerous for infants. Baby could choke from her formula coming too fast from that propped bottle. She could also choke on milk curds if she should spit up. She might be unable to clear her throat.

Start with the Kitchen

Dangers multiply rapidly when your child is crawling, then walking. Accident-proofing involves far more now that he can plunge so quickly into risky situations.

The kitchen is a marvelous learning laboratory for babies and toddlers. Designing it so it's safe for your baby is an important challenge. Hazards in many kitchens include:

- Cleaning supplies (Don't keep them in the cupboard under your sink.)
- Knives
- Vegetable grater
- Ice pick
- Cooking fork
- Hot pans (Keep the handles turned toward the back of the stove.)
- Coffee pot, toaster, and other appliance cords
- Iron and ironing board (Iron when baby is asleep, then put board and iron away.)
- Gas stove with controls baby can reach

During the years you have a baby or young child, it is terribly important that you put such dangerous items in a high cupboard. Even there, if he's a climber, you should use a secure lock.

> ### Warning
> If baby gets dishwashing detergent on his fingers, he'll put them in his mouth as usual. Because dishwashing detergent is so powerful, it can burn his mouth badly. Don't let it happen!

Toddlers may turn on the hot water faucet. Be sure the water temperature is low enough not to scald baby.

When your child has a minor accident such as touching the stove and burning his fingers slightly, help him

understand what happened. Don't say anything about "the
bad stove" burning him, and don't fix it up with cookies.
Sympathize, of course, and put ice on the burn. Also explain if he touches the stove when it's hot, he'll be burned.

Gas Stove Is Risky

If you're buying a range, you may be able to get one
with controls on top at the back. If the controls are in
baby's reach, you'll have to watch constantly that he
doesn't turn the burner on. A gas stove without a self-
lighting device is extremely dangerous in a home with little
children. If it's turned on, but not lit, unburned gas will
escape into the room. This could cause an explosion or
asphyxiate people (cause them to stop breathing).

If you have a gas heater, have someone help you check if
it has a safety valve that shuts off the gas if the pilot light
goes out. If it doesn't have one and the pilot goes out, the
escaping unburned gas is toxic and can cause an explosion.

The baby should not be left in a room with an unvented
gas heater because the gas (burned or unburned) will stay in
the room rather than going up a chimney or stack. Call your
gas company if you don't know whether your heater is
vented. For the same reason, you should not heat a room by
leaving a gas oven door open.

If you ever smell gas in your home, check with the gas
company immediately. In most areas, they will send
someone out to check it at no charge to you.

Other Hazards

Sonja pulls on the tablecloth. If it were my own
home, I wouldn't leave it on the table. People tell me
kids have to learn not to touch it. I think when they're
babies, you can't do that.

                                    Julie, 16 - Sonja, 7 months

To a creeping baby, tablecloths are to be pulled. If hot foods, even empty dishes, come down with the cloth, results can be disastrous. Even placemats can cause big problems. Our second son, when he was eleven months old, pulled on a placemat early one winter morning. Over came the cup of freshly poured coffee. Steve's burn required emergency hospital treatment.

You know how baby loves to play peek-a-boo by putting a blanket over his face. He might do the same thing if he found a thin plastic bag. If he did, he could suffocate within minutes. The plastic would cling to his face, and he wouldn't be able to breathe.

Carefully keep all plastic of this kind away from your baby. Cut up and discard such bags immediately after you get them, especially those put on the clothes at the dry cleaner's.

Even if you lock up all medicines, you may decide the bathroom is one room your baby can't enter. If she can't open doors herself, just keep the door shut at all times. Make it as safe as possible inside, however, because you know she will get in there occasionally.

During the time she is pulling herself to stand, be especially careful to keep the bathroom door closed. It's possible for a toddler to pull herself up by the edge of the toilet, lose her balance, fall in, and drown.

The day will come when your toddler goes into the bathroom herself. She may even lock the door behind her. A lock-release on the outside of the bathroom door would solve that problem. Keep the release key where you can find it quickly.

You might also decide to put a hook and eye closure on the outside of the bathroom door. Install it so high that your child can't reach it. When the door is hooked shut, you know baby won't go in.

Older sister's toys can be dangerous to baby.

Check All Areas for Danger

I had to buy a gate to block the stairs when Dono-
van started crawling. We covered up all the sockets,
and I shut the doors in the bathrooms because he'd
run in there and flush the toilet over and over.

Belia, 17 - Donovan, 2

Stairs are an obvious danger to a creeping/crawling/
toddling child. Putting a gate at the top and one at the
bottom is a solution. Put the lower gate at the second or
third step up, not at the bottom. Baby will then have a
chance to practice climbing a few steps, then coming back
down. He won't have far enough to fall to hurt himself,
especially if there's a soft rug at the bottom.

It takes pretty constant watching where I'm living.
Quentin (Heidi's uncle) leaves little screws and things
on the floor in his bedroom. I've asked him a few
times to pick them up, but he doesn't. I get furious and
start yelling at him.

Jenny, 18 - Heidi, 13 months

Another room you may decide to shut off, perhaps with a gate, is where an older brother or sister plays. Satisfying baby's curiosity there might cause more trouble with big sister than it's worth. If big sister is only a few years older, she can't be expected to understand completely what child-proofing means. Besides, big sister should not be expected to share her things, particularly not without her permission.

If you have a fireplace, open heater, heating register, or floor furnace, put guards in front of and over it. Use furniture to block off radiators.

Has your toddler learned to open doors? As mentioned earlier, you can attach fasteners, the hook-and-eye kind, up too high for him to reach. You'll need some method of keeping doors closed if they lead to stairways, driveways, and some storage areas.

Your window and door screens should be securely fastened. If your house has bars on the windows, they need to be the kind that can be opened from the inside.

Sometimes I'll be doing something, curling my hair or polishing my nails. Next thing I know, Heidi's gone out the doggy door, and is playing with the dogs in the back yard. I'll bring her back, and she'll do it again.

Jenny

Do you have a pet door, a little door your dog or cat can open? If it's big enough for your baby to get through, expect him to use it!

Accident-Proof Outside Areas

If you have a swimming pool, be sure it's fenced securely with a *locked* gate. Tragically, many small children die in family swimming pools each year.

If you live in an apartment complex with a pool, and you find the gate left open, report it to the manager. A toddler and a swimming pool can be a deadly combination.

A fenced-in yard is a marvelous luxury for a toddler and her parents. If you're lucky enough to have one, enjoy it, but keep an eye on your child as she plays there.

Yards, fenced or not, and garages need to be child-proofed, too. Check for rubbish, insecticides, paint removers, and other poisons. Get rid of them or lock them up. Nails, screws, and other hardware, assorted car parts, tools, and gardening equipment should be stored out of reach or locked in the garage.

Also get rid of rusty or tippy furniture. Check hammocks, swings, and other play equipment regularly for safety.

One time a year or two ago Dalton fell off a lawn chair and smacked his head against the sidewalk, and he had three bumps. We rushed him to the emergency room, but he was okay.

He was sitting there rocking himself on the chair, and I said, "If you keep that up, you'll fall." And he did.

                                    Claire, 17 - Dalton, 33 months

You don't want to be overly protective to the point that your child is afraid to climb anything. It might be wiser, however, to calmly remove him from the tippy chair. Then explain to him why you don't want him up there. This works better than saying crossly, "If you keep that up, you'll fall."

Some plants are poisonous such as poinsettia, caster beans, and oleander. Does your yard have shrubbery or other plants dangerous to your child? Also check any house plants in your home.

Even a lovely rose garden can harm a toddler when she runs into all those thorns. Putting a temporary, but sturdy fence around your roses will protect baby. It will also protect the roses.

Is Paint Lead-Free?

Do you have furniture, walls, or woodwork in your home which were painted before 1970? If the paint contains lead, it can damage your child if he chews on the painted surface, or if the paint is peeling and he puts bits of it in his mouth. Lead poisoning can be the result, a serious problem for babies and children.

Even though more recent coats of paint in old houses are probably lead-free, chips of paint can include the bottom layers of lead-base paint. Many children eat these chips of peeling paint and plaster. Apparently they taste sweet, and children like them.

Glazed ceramic dishes imported from other countries may have lead in the glaze, lead which may contaminate food cooked or served in the dish.

If children get too much lead, they show signs of lead poisoning. "Too much" for a baby may be a very little bit of the paint. The child may become anemic and lose his appetite. He may be either listless or hyperactive and irritable. He may find it harder to learn, and may suffer convulsions and permanent brain damage from the poisoning.

If you suspect lead poisoning, check with your health-care provider. Through a simple blood test, she can detect the condition. If lead poisoning has occurred, the doctor can recommend treatment to get rid of much of the extra lead in your child's body so he won't have the problems described above.

Car Safety

Of course you'll do everything you can to keep your toddler from running out into the street. But did you know

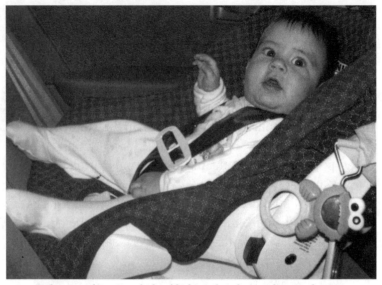

Baby must be securely buckled in when he's riding in the car.

that more children are hurt *inside* cars as passengers than
are injured on the outside as pedestrians?

Traffic accidents are the leading cause of death in
childhood once the critical early months have passed. They
claim more lives than any disease. In addition, hundreds of
thousands of children are injured each year. Many remain
permanently disabled, physically and/or mentally.

You can protect your child from injury while riding in
your car by putting him in a safety-approved car seat (not a
car bed).

For infants, you need a seat in which the baby rides
facing backward in a semi-reclining position. It should be
held firmly in place by the car's seat belt. Children should
ride in a rear-facing car seat until they are a year old and
weigh at least twenty pounds.

When you choose a car seat for toddlers and slightly
older children, too, be sure the seat can be fastened securely
by the car's seat belt. In most states, babies and toddlers are

required by law to be fastened in a car seat when riding in a car.

A car seat, of course, is safe only if the child is buckled in it. When your toddler decides to be negative about his car seat, it's time for you to be positive. Fasten him in it matter-of-factly, even if he's screaming. Be sure he knows you and others in the car use seat belts, too.

Safety — A Big Responsibility

You can do everything possible to safety-proof your home, but what about the dangers outside your home? Can you do anything about that? Samantha feels strongly about this issue:

Now with a child, you won't catch me partying, you won't catch me smoking. Having her changed me. Some of the girls with two kids say they're still in their gang, and they're proud. You're in a gang, you're a bullet target, and so is your kid.

If somebody did something with my child, or I was at the wrong place at the wrong time, and they started shooting, I would cover my daughter. I would let them get me before they get her.

A lot of people have told me, "You should get in a gang." Why? So I can be crippled? I want to be up there running with my child, have fun with my child.
Samantha, 16 - Kaylie, 20 months

Making sure your child is safe in your home, in your car, everywhere he goes, is a big responsibility. Creating a safe environment that also allows him to explore and to learn about his world is a double challenge with double rewards.

You will find more peace of mind knowing your child is not in danger, and you will be delighted with the bright, happy individual that he is.

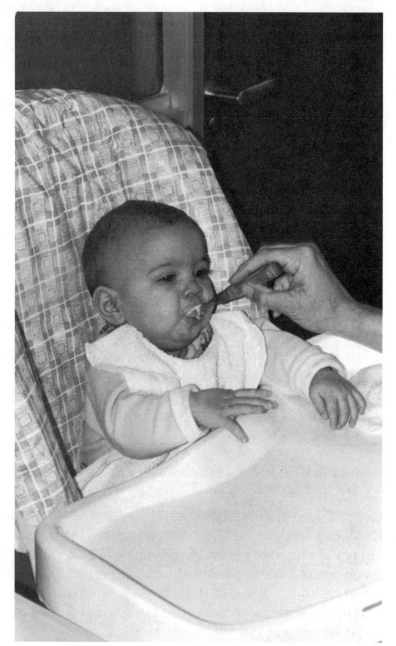

At six months he's ready for some solid food.

10

Baby's First Solid Food

- **Don't Rush Solid Food**
- **Solids by Six Months**
- **Vegetables, Fruits for Baby**
- **You Can Fix It Yourself**
- **Cook and Freeze**
- **Finger Food for Baby**
- **Drinking from a Cup**
- **When He Feeds Himself**

I waited about five months to give Nick solid foods. He likes to be nursed after he eats, and then he falls asleep. I used to leak, and I wanted to nurse him, but at this point I think it's best to feed him solids first.

I give him cereal in the morning, then bring him here to the center where I nurse him.

Theresa, 16 - Nick, 6 months

I broil hamburger and put it in the blender with a little bit of formula. When we have chicken for dinner, I put it in the blender, or I give her the drumstick to chew on.

Julie, 16 - Sonja, 7 months

Don't Rush Solid Food

Your baby doesn't need solid food and generally shouldn't have it until he's at least four or five months old. Almost all babies get along best on breast milk or formula during this time.

If you feed your baby solids too soon, he is more likely:

• to develop food allergies.

• to have digestive problems.

Feeding solids to a tiny baby is usually time-consuming and often frustrating to mother and to baby. Mother spoons it in, baby rolls it right back out! Before he's four months old, baby has a well-developed sucking reflex. He sucks before he swallows his formula or breast milk. Food put in his mouth from a spoon is usually spit right back out. This is called the protrusion reflex.

By about four months of age, this protrusion reflex is gone, and he's much more able to accept food on his tongue. He can swallow it instead of letting it roll back out. It's as if he's saying during those early months, "Mom, I don't want solid food!"

In addition, if you buy strained (Stage 1) baby food, the cost can be rather high — high, at least, when you realize this is money spent which gives no benefit to baby during these early months. So why do so many parents start feeding cereal and other solids to their very young baby? They may have several reasons. First, they may think feeding him cereal in the evening will make baby sleep through the night. Research shows this is simply not true.

Sometimes people you love, perhaps your own mother, urge you to start early feeding. The research which shows that babies are better off without early solid food is fairly new. A generation or two ago, neither doctors nor the rest of us realized that early feeding can, and often does, cause allergies and stomach upsets.

When my children were babies, we thought we should start giving them cereal when they were only a few weeks old. As a result, Steve (one of my sons) has a lot of trouble with allergies. Steve and I both wish I had known to delay the solid food.

Even your doctor may tell you it's okay to start feeding solids to baby when he's very young. If this happens, talk to him. Some healthcare providers seem to think all mothers want to rush solid feeding. After discussing it, you and your doctor may agree baby doesn't need cereal yet, and that it's all right to wait until he's at least four months old.

Solids by Six Months

I gave Sujatha baby cereal and fruits and juices when she was five months old. She started with rice cereal, but she didn't like it the first time. She made a huge mess — her hands were in it as I fed her.

Kimiko, 17 - Sujatha, 5 months

Ideally, then, you don't feed baby solid food for at least four months. It's important, however, that you do start spoon-feeding her and giving her finger foods by the time she's six months old. Reasons to feed solid food to baby by six months include:

* She needs nutrients she isn't getting from breast milk or formula.
* She needs to learn to eat solids, a quite different process from getting her food through sucking.
* Four to six months seems to be the ideal age to help baby learn this new method of eating. By this time it's also important that she learn to eat a variety of foods.

Start with infant rice cereal. Use the dry, iron-enriched kind that you buy in a box. Rice is less likely to cause

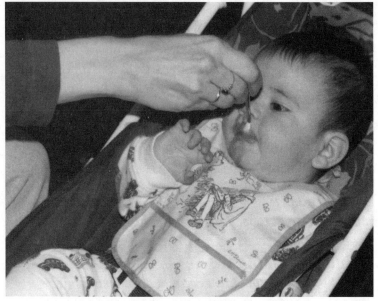

Eating is serious business.

allergies than other kinds of cereal such as wheat. Above
all, don't start with the mixed cereal. If she's allergic to just
one of the ingredients, you won't know which one it is.
Mix the dry rice cereal with a little formula. If you're
breastfeeding, you can pump enough milk for her cereal at
first. She'll be more willing to accept the cereal if it smells
and tastes somewhat like her formula or breast milk. Mix
enough liquid with the cereal to make it quite thin at first.

Carefully choose the "right" time for teaching baby to
eat solid food. Don't attempt spoon-feeding at first when
she's terribly hungry. She would be furious at the delay in
getting the bottle or breast she wants.

She needs to be reasonably hungry or she won't bother
trying this new food. About half-through her breast- or
bottle-feeding is usually the best time.

A small, narrow, shallow-bowled spoon with a fairly
long handle works best for these early feedings. To baby,

eating from a regular teaspoon feels like eating from a huge tablespoon would feel to us. (Try it sometime. You'll see why she needs a little spoon to match her mouth size.)

If baby doesn't sit up by herself yet, put her in your lap or in her infant seat for her first solid food experience. She needs to be a little more upright than for her breast- or bottle-feeding.

Next step is for you to relax! If she doesn't like cereal the first time, that's okay. Try again tomorrow — and the next day. If she still resists, wait a few days before trying again. If she swallows a bit of cereal, congratulate her. Be thrilled. Show her you're pleased. If she doesn't eat it, don't make a big deal of it.

Warning

Sometimes parents mix cereal and formula together, then feed it to baby from a bottle. *Don't!* Your baby needs to learn to eat from a spoon. An infant feeder which practically "injects" the food into her mouth is bad, too. *Don't buy it.*

Let her drink formula and water from a bottle. Help her learn that solid foods are eaten from a spoon. Fairly soon she will also learn about finger foods.

Vegetables, Fruits for Baby

Start feeding baby vegetables, fruits, and their juices sometime between his fifth and seventh month. Traditionally, babies have eaten white fruits first, usually applesauce or pears, perhaps because almost all babies like the taste. After the sweet taste of fruit, however, baby may balk at vegetables. You may decide to start with a vegetable, perhaps squash, sweet potatoes, or carrots.

Mashed banana is often one of the first foods given to

baby. Most babies like it, and it's super-easy to mash to a
smooth consistency. You *don't* need to buy it in a jar!

If you decide to buy Stage 1 baby food, read the labels
carefully before you buy. Choose basic fruits, vegetables,
and strained meats.

Don't buy combination meals because you get less
protein per serving with them than you would if you mixed
together a jar of meat and a jar of vegetables yourself.

If the label tells you the food contains a lot of sugar and
modified starches, don't buy it.

Skip the baby desserts because baby doesn't need them
any more than the rest of us do.

You Can Fix It Yourself

He eats real food now — chicken, vegetables,
carrots. I steam them, then put them in a grinder or
mash them. He eats table food, Chicken McNuggets.
He eats with us when we go out.

Ynez, 16 - Lenny, 7 months

Fixing food for baby is easy. If you have a blender, use
it. Or you can buy a baby food grinder for just a few dollars. With it, you prepare small amounts of food for baby.
The blender is easier for fixing larger amounts, and works
better during the short time baby needs very smooth,
strained or Stage 1 food.

Important vitamins are lost when you cook foods in
boiling water. The steam method of cooking will save more
of those vitamins. The food is held above the boiling water
so it will cook only in the steam.

A steam basket, available in most department stores, fits
into most pans. You need to use a pan with a tight-fitting
lid. Many adults prefer steamed vegetables because foods
cooked this way retain more natural flavor.

If you're cooking for the whole family, be sure to take

baby's portion out *before* you add salt, sugar, and other seasonings. She won't mind. A craving for extra salt is learned by eating foods with added salt. Don't season her food to meet your taste. You're fixing it for your baby, not yourself. Too much salt in one's diet can cause numerous health problems including hypertension. Eating sugar may cause a craving for sweets, and is hard on her teeth. Help your baby avoid these problems by having as little salt and sugar as possible in her diet.

If possible, use your family's meals as a start. If you're having a vegetable, put a small amount (without seasonings) through a baby food grinder. Perhaps you're having a meat that is also suitable for blending. Do you like applesauce? If so, share it with baby.

Cook and Freeze

If your family meals aren't suitable for baby, you can still prepare her food without spending a great deal of time. Best approach is to cook and freeze ahead. See recipes on page 144.

Simply pour prepared food into ice cube trays. Freeze it quickly, keeping protein food, vegetables, and fruits separate. Then store the cubes in plastic freezer bags or in reusable containers. Be sure to label and date the food you're freezing. Use it within two months.

With a little planning, you can have a nice variety of food stored in your freezer. If you fix a different vegetable for your family each night one week, simply cook at least twice the amount you need. Prepare the extra amount for baby, then freeze. Do the same with fruits. You may find it easier than running to the store to buy jars of baby food.

When you're ready to serve the cubes, thaw in a warming dish or in an egg-poaching cup over boiling water. The

Recipes for Baby

Cooked Fruit

- Wash, peel, and cut apples, peaches, pears, plums, or apricots into small pieces. Remove pits.
- Simmer or steam until tender (10-20 minutes). Don't add sugar.
- Using baby food grinder or blender, blend until smooth.
- You can also buy fruit canned in water or its own juices, no sugar added. Grind or blend as above.

Cooked Vegetables

- Simmer cut-up vegetables in one inch of water, or steam over boiling water until tender.
- Mash or blend the vegetables.
- Add cooking water to get the right consistency.
- You can also buy vegetables canned in water without seasonings. Grind or blend as above.

Meat for Baby

- Use meat you've cooked for your family.
- Blend to a smooth consistency.
- Add a little water, broth, or juice as needed.

* Uncooked Fruit

- Wash and peel an apple, pear, peach, or apricot.
- Add a little water. Blend.
- * NOTE: Offer only after six months of age.

little individual egg-poaching pan is a convenient size, and is relatively inexpensive.

You don't need to warm the food beyond room temperature. Baby's taste buds are not fully developed, and what seems warm to you may seem hot to baby.

If you wait until he's six months old to start baby on solid food, you'll need to use blended/Stage 1 food for only a couple of months. He can be eating table food, much of it mashed, by the time he's eight months old.

Even if you don't want to prepare smoothly blended baby food yourself, you surely won't buy jars of Stage 2 or Stage 3 food. Feeding him from the family meals is so little bother to you, and it's better for baby. Simply put food through a baby food grinder until he's ready to chew the real stuff.

Finger food to study — and to eat.

At first, offer baby only one new food each week. If he's allergic to that food, if he gets a rash or seems to have a digestion problem, you'll know that particular food is probably causing the problem. If you fed him a new food each day, you wouldn't have any idea which one to remove.

Finger Food for Baby

Give him finger foods as early as he can handle them. By the time he's six or seven months old, he can pick up small slices of banana or Cheerios. Before long he'll be ready for graham crackers, pieces of toast, teething biscuits, even little bits of meat and cheese.

Plain, unsweetened Cheerios are a marvelous early food-toy. He'll pick one up in each hand, look at it, stick it in his mouth. They contain some nutrition and, most important, are very low in sugar.

Don't give him sugar cereals. Such "cereals" should be labeled breakfast candy. Some are actually more than half sugar!

Your baby can probably:

• Hold and gum a teething biscuit by five months.

• Handle little pieces of hard-boiled egg yolk (no egg white yet) by six months.

• Eat dry unsugared cereal, soft toast, French toast, cooked carrot and potato pieces, peas with skins broken, even diced liverwurst sandwiches by seven months.

He can handle all these things himself by eating with his fingers.

Drinking from a Cup

I'm trying to give Orlando a bottle occasionally, but he doesn't want one. He does good already with a cup. He holds on to it, and he can take it right to his mouth although his coordination isn't very good yet.

Holly, 17 - Orlando, 5 months

When she's five or six months old, offer baby a little formula or juice in a cup. You can buy a cup with a lid and a spout as a bridge between bottle and cup. Before long, she'll be able to drink a little formula, water, and juice from her cup.

Nick is learning to drink from a cup. Yesterday I gave him a training cup, and he's learning how to use it. He eats flour tortillas. He eats crackers and holds them himself.

Theresa, 16 - Nick, 6 months

When He Feeds Himself

Learning to eat solid food is an exciting milestone for baby, and for you. As long as you don't rush the process, you both can enjoy the experience.

For two or three months, preparing his food (or perhaps buying jars of prepared Stage 1 food) is another task you do for your baby. Feeding him provides more togetherness. Keeping mealtime pleasant is important.

Sometimes he won't want that new food you're serving him . . . perhaps because he isn't hungry, or maybe he doesn't like it. This is not the time to force him to eat. In fact, insisting he eat when he doesn't want to is never a good policy (unless necessary for medical reasons).

This is the time he starts learning that a variety of foods are good. He also learns that eating can be a loving time whether he's breastfeeding, drinking from a bottle, or eating solid food.

By the time he's about eight months old, he'll be able to eat the fruits and vegetables, bread and cereals, and some of the meats you eat. Of course you'll need to mash/chop them for him for awhile yet, but he won't need completely smooth food — and you won't need to buy jars of baby food. Instead, he'll learn to eat "real" food.

Your baby is growing rapidly — soon she'll be a toddler!

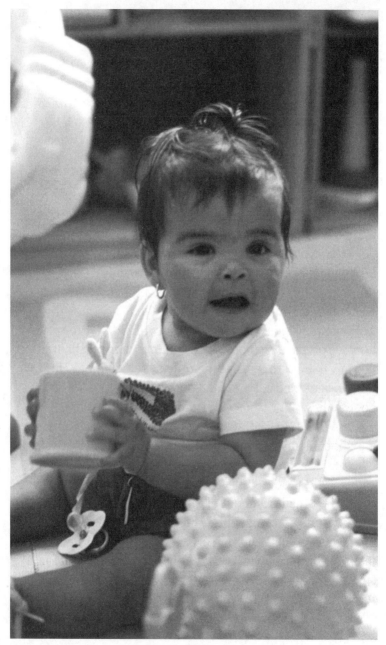

She's delighted when you play with her.

11

Playing with Your Baby

- **Simple Toys Are Best**
- **Time for Games**
- **Walkers? Playpens? No!**
- **She Likes Mirrors**
- **He Listens and "Talks"**
- **Continue Talking to Baby**
- **Reading Is Important**
- **Self-Esteem Is Crucial**

What I like about him is he's fun. He's real playful with almost everybody. You play with him just a little bit and he'll smile a lot. He always has a smile on his face. People say he looks like me.

I like taking him with me to the park when I go there with my friends to play handball. There are four or five of my friends at my house every day. They help me out a lot.

Andy 17 - Gus 5 months

I play with Orlando — clap my hands, play patty-cake, sing to him, talk to him. He holds his head up now. He doesn't like to

play by himself yet, so I lie on the floor with him.
When he gets bored, I squeak the toys for him. He
plays with his feet when he's in the infant seat.
He loves to chew because he's teething. He's
hanging on to things pretty well, and he chews on
everything.

Holly, 17 - Orlando, 5 months

Simple Toys Are Best

Buchanan has toys, and he enjoys playing by
himself. He has that security. I play with him some,
but I want him to be able to have his own indepen-
dence, too. I've already seen that in him.

Camelia, 16 - Buchanan, 6 months

Your little pre-walker may often play alone for as long as
an hour *if* mother or dad is nearby. Talk to her as you work.
Give her a different object to play with every once
in awhile.

Collect small objects for your child to play with and to
explore. Let her spend a lot of time on the floor on a blanket. In front of her, put several small items and a container
for them. Choose things that are two to five inches in size,
and with a variety of shapes and textures. She'll spend a lot
of time exploring these objects and practicing simple skills
with them.

These small objects don't need to be expensive toys.
She'll undoubtedly prefer items from your kitchen drawers.
For example:

• Plastic measuring spoons and cups

• Shiny can of sardines (Remove key from can.)

• Plastic freezer container

• Big pan

Put everything in the big pan, and she'll be delighted.

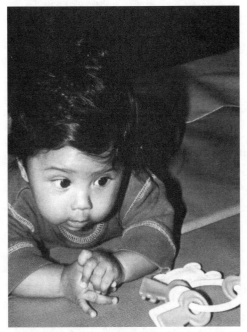
*Now he can pick something up
and carefully examine it.*

She'll look at each thing as she takes it out of the pan. She'll feel it and chew it. She may bang things together.

Be sure the items you offer her are safe. The handle on a wooden spoon or even some pan handles can be dangerous if she falls on them.

When she's tired of these things, you'll find more in your kitchen. Just be sure each thing you give her is smooth and safe for her. Nothing should be smaller than 11/2 inches. Remember, anything you give her will be mouthed if at all possible.

Nick likes a plastic bottle and other containers. I cleaned out one container and put little rocks in it, and he loves that. Of course I taped the lid on tight.
Theresa, 16 - Nick, 6 months

Sometime during this stage, baby will be ready for simple stacking toys. You can give her plastic cups that will nest. Be sure they don't stick together.

Time for Games

Sonja loves to play peek-a-boo. My mom says to play it with her a lot because it's like me disappearing,

*and then coming back. She'll hold covers over her
face, then drop them. I'll say "Boo!" and she'll laugh.
Or we'll play peek-a-boo around the corner.*

Julie, 16 - Sonja, 7 months

Even though baby can now play alone, give him attention when he's happily occupied as well as when he's
fussing. As he plays, talk to him, throw him a kiss, hug him
as you walk by. Smiling often at him will be easy. He'll
love to play games with you. Give him a few minutes of
your time several times a day for games.

Make a game out of baby learning to use one thing to get
another. Sit on the floor with your baby. Put a small blanket
in front of him. Put a toy on the blanket, but out of your
child's reach. Show your child how to get the toy by
pulling on the blanket. Can he do it himself?

*I put Kolbee on a blanket down on the floor, and he
tries to grab his rattles. Then it gets underneath him,
and that upsets him. I just pull it out, and then he's
happy again.*

*I make faces at him, and make him laugh. I stand
him up, and he likes that.*

*I talk to Kolbee a lot. I used to say I didn't know
what to say to him, but now I just say anything. When
he sees me coming, he gets happier. He gets a kick out
of everything.*

Vanessa, 17 - Kolbee, 5 months

Specific games with baby are fun, but at this stage, they
need take only a few minutes. Patty-cake and peek-a-boo
are the old standbys.

Baby will enjoy going outdoors with you. If he isn't
crawling yet, lay him on a blanket near you while you work
in your yard.

When he starts crawling, let him play in the grass. A

little dirt won't hurt him. You need to watch him rather closely, of course.

Sunshine is lovely, and provides some vitamin D for your child if his skin is exposed to it. Too much sunshine is harmful.

Babies should have very limited doses of sun. Start out with two minutes of sun a day, front and back. Don't expose baby to midday sun in the hot summer. Sunning sessions should be before 10 a.m. and after 3 p.m. Be sure to protect your baby's eyes from the sun.

If you take your baby or toddler to the beach, you'll need an umbrella unless you're staying for only a few minutes.

Walkers? Playpens? No!

During the early part of this stage, your child may still use her infant seat. Place her in the seat near you so she can watch you work. Be sure you set her in a safe place on the floor.

As soon as she can sit up by herself, however, she won't want to sit in it. By that time, she probably would not be safe in it, either. She might be able to tip it over.

People used to put babies in walkers, but old style (ring) walkers are not safe for baby. Also, if a baby spends a lot of time in his walker, walking on his own will be delayed. Crawling is an important foundation for walking.

Playpens are also used by many families. If you take a poll on your street, you'll probably find several babies caged in playpens. In fact, some babies put up with spending several hours a day in a playpen.

A playpen is a handy item to take to the beach. A seven-month-old baby is not ready to be turned loose in the sand. At home, the playpen can be a safe and fun place for a baby for perhaps ten minutes — long enough for you to take a shower.

Baby won't learn much if he's stuck in a playpen.

Playpens are all right, but not for a long period of time. I would feel caged in if I had that little area. But when I'm cleaning the house, sometimes I put Sonja in there for a little while. It gets hard trying to do something now that she goes everywhere.

When she's playing in her playpen and she gets restless, I put that picture of me right outside her playpen. Sonja looks at it and gets quiet. My sister started that, and it was a great idea. Or I put a big mirror outside the playpen.

Julie

Babies generally are bored in playpens. Some scream until you let them out. Others may not fuss so much, especially if they have been stuck in their pen since they were tiny. But how much do you learn when you're bored? Not much! Your bored baby doesn't learn much either. If you use a playpen, do so as little as possible. Your baby needs to be able to satisfy her curiosity. She will learn so much more playing with you, being near you as you work, than she possibly could learn off by herself in a playpen.

Arranging her environment so she can have freedom to explore is part of your job as a parent. Baby will appreciate your efforts. Chapter 9 offered suggestions on baby-proofing your house so you and baby can survive her creeping/toddling months with as little frustration as possible. Making your home as accident-proof as you can is part of parenting.

She Likes Mirrors

I've held Kerry up to the mirror. She looks, and wonders what's going on. She's able to distinguish me from her. She knows who she is, but she isn't sure what to think of two mommies.

Leslie, 20 - Amy, 27 months; Kerry, 4 months

Babies love mirrors. Hold your baby in front of a full-length mirror and watch his reaction. He may be puzzled at seeing you there, apparently a second you. His own reflection will intrigue him because he will soon learn he can make that "person" move when he moves.

One of the best "toys" for this age is an unbreakable mirror placed six or seven inches from baby's eyes. Glass mirrors are dangerous. Look for a good quality plastic mirror four or five inches in diameter. If it isn't fairly good quality, his image will be distorted.

He Listens and "Talks"

*I talk to Gary, and he goos back at me. He looks at
my mouth, then tries to copy my expressions and what
I do with my mouth.*

Leica, 18 - Gary, 3 months

By two or three months, baby will hear a sound, then
look to see where it's coming from. Sometime during this
stage, the sound of your footsteps coming toward her room
may quiet her while she watches for you. She may enjoy
soothing music, although she undoubtedly prefers the
sound of your voice singing to her.

Baby is becoming much more active now. It's even more
important that you talk to her, but *talk* to her, don't lecture.
Hold a dialog even though she doesn't answer in words.
Ask questions, then pause for her answer. That's how she
learns about speech patterns. Before long she'll be
responding to you with her brand of talking.

*Carol plays with her saliva, makes sounds by
spitting it out. I heard her say Da-da once, I really
did. I screamed and ran to get Mario, but she hasn't
done it since.*

Kristyn, 17 - Carol, 3 months

Don't use "baby talk" with her. She will learn faster if
she hears words pronounced correctly. Learning baby talk
is not what she needs. She wants to talk like you do.

Continue Talking to Baby

*Kerry is talked to all the time. We have two other
people living here, and I take her over to my mom's
about three times a week. Everybody talks to her. I
like talking to her because she smiles.*

Leslie

Baby will begin to understand a few words now. He may even say "Ma-ma," "Da-da," and "Bye," but don't count on it. What you can count on is his ability to make delightful sounds. You'll hear him in his crib "talking."

When I talk with her, Sancia looks right at me and acts like she's hearing what I'm saying. She likes it when people play with her. When I change her, I look at her, and I talk with her.

One time, when she was in her crib, I thought she was crying. I went in, and she was lying there making little sounds, talking to herself.

Emilia, 17 - Sancia, 6 months

This is a beautiful time to put a tape recorder by his crib. Try to turn it on just before you think he'll wake up. If you walk in to see him, however, his jabbering will stop because your face and voice are even more interesting to him than the sounds he's making himself.

Your child needs you to help him develop language. You need to talk to him and read to him long before he learns to talk himself. It's especially important now to talk about the things he knows. As you change his diaper, talk about it. As you dress him, say, "Now I'm putting your shoe on your foot. Your hand goes through your sleeve." Name the parts of his body as you bathe him. Talk about the toys you're handing him.

I talk to Nick all the time. My mom talks to him, and so does my dad. He's very talkative — maybe he takes after me. We've all talked to him since he was tiny. Maybe that's why he's usually happy.

Theresa

As you carry baby around the house, show him different objects. Name and describe such things as chair, door,

table, dish, picture, TV, couch. Take him outdoors, and
name the sidewalk, tree, fence, grass. As you do this again
and again, he'll learn a lot about his world. He'll enjoy
your attention, too. Different sounds, such as music, an
airplane, a dog barking, interest him.
Sometimes when you're talking to baby, whisper in his
ear. He'll enjoy the change, and he'll learn to listen to
different levels of speech.

Reading Is Important

*Carlos loves his books. He'll sit there and look at
the books and talk to them. I told him the story of the
Three Bears, and he liked it.*

Renette, 16 - Carlos , 6 months

If you aren't already reading to your baby, start now.
Choose very simple stories, preferably with pictures of
things he knows. At this age, you may have trouble getting
his attention.

Reading (mostly looking at pictures) at bedtime is ideal.
If baby is sleepy, he'll be more willing to sit still for a
story. If he sits or lies still long enough for a story, he'll be
more likely to go to bed without causing a lot of
commotion.

*I read to Jay at night after I give him his bath. It
calms him down a little.*

Bev, 17 - Jay, 8 months

You don't need to buy all of baby's books. You can make
them yourself. Cut big colorful pictures out of magazines.
Choose pictures of things familiar to baby such as a cat,
puppy, or car. Pictures of babies will fascinate him. Paste
the pictures on cardboard. Punch holes in the "pages," and
tie together with brightly colored yarn.

Or you may want to invest in an inexpensive photograph

album, the kind with plastic over the pages. The plastic has adhesive already on it to hold the pictures in place. After you put in the pictures and relay the plastic, tape down all loose edges carefully with cellophane tape.

Again, choose pictures of subjects that are of particular interest to your child.

Self-Esteem Is Crucial

Juan plays on the floor while I do the dishes. I'll turn to him every couple of minutes and say his name, and I think he's beginning to know it. I don't ever call him names like Fathead, because when he gets bigger, he'd believe it. When he burps, I always say, "Good boy."

Ginny, 17 - Juan, 4 months

Self-esteem is extremely important to all of us. Parents must think well of themselves before they can truly think well of their baby. To feel good about someone else, you start out by feeling good about yourself.

You can help your baby gain a good sense of self-esteem. Whenever she does something different, learns a new skill, cheer her on. If she bats at an object and manages to hit it, praise her. When she can finally grab that object, get excited with her.

Calling a baby "Stupid" or some other put-down word can too easily turn into a "self-fulfilling prophecy."

Self-fulfilling prophecy: Something that happens because one expects it to happen.

If you tell him often enough that he's stupid, he will decide he must indeed be stupid. If he thinks he can't learn well, he probably won't. Of course you won't do that to your child. Babies come equipped with a delightful urge to learn.

Watch the baby who has just learned to turn from her back to her stomach. She will practice her new skill over and over and over again. She'll be thrilled each time she does so. Being able to do something today that she couldn't do yesterday excites her — especially if you're exited, too, and you show her you are.

As you play with your baby, as you talk and read to him, you'll both have a good time. In addition, all this interaction with him is helping his brain develop. Because you play with him, he is likely to be a smarter baby!

You have a wonderful challenge as you nurture your baby's zest for life, learning, and excitement. *Enjoy!*

Part IV
Leaving
Baby Stage Behind

Sometime during the last four months of your child's first year, he will probably crawl. He may even be walking by his birthday. One thing is almost certain. He will get around at a surprisingly rapid pace.

Child-proofing your house is a big challenge at this stage. With intensive child-proofing, you make your home safe for and safe from your exploring child.

Your baby may be joining you at the table for at least some of her meals. By now she can eat many of the things you eat if you simply mash or chop the food into manageable bites. See chapter 13 for more information.

Your child continues to learn amazingly quickly. You're his teacher as you play with him, talk with him, and read to him. Chapter 14 includes more on this topic including several toys you can make.

The last chapter focuses on your future, or rather, your and your baby's future together. How do you prepare for the self-sufficient life you want? It's an important topic.

He can crawl — and he's taking off.

12

He's into Everything!

Gary has been walking since he was ten months old. He says "Mama," "Pa-pa." We talk to him a lot in both English and Spanish. He's curious. If he sees you doing something, he copies you. He'll come over and look. He's very close to me.

He climbs up on a board, and then jumps off, but he's not on the couches yet. He loves playing outside with other kids.

He takes pans out of the cupboard and takes them outside. He picks up a lot of rocks and puts them in the pans and carries them around.

Jan, 15 - Gary, 12 months

Robin's a monster. She gets into everything. She's crawling around, pulling herself up, standing up, grabbing all sorts of things.

Melinda, 15 - Robin, 9 months

Difficult Stage for Parents

This is the busiest stage yet for both you and your child. She no longer is an infant. She's finally able to move, and move she will. Soon, in fact, she may be running.

Shareef started crawling when she was eight months old. She got into everything. She loves going in the kitchen and playing with the pans. Whatever she finds, she puts in her mouth, and it's real hard. Whenever she sees a door, she tries to get out.

Adia, 17 - Shareef, 11 months

This is a difficult stage for many parents. "She gets into everything," they say. Because she can get into so many things, people assume she should be able to understand wrong from right. She should be able to follow your orders.

This isn't true. Her memory is only beginning to develop. If she does happen to remember that you said "No" the last time she touched that fragile glass vase, she still doesn't have the self-control to leave such an inviting item alone. Slapping her hand mostly teaches her that big people hit little people. She really doesn't know why.

At this point, removing her from temptation is the smart and loving approach. You can offer her a safe toy or activity instead of the forbidden one. Chances are pretty good that she'll accept the change.

Learning Through Curiosity

Every parent has a huge responsibility to make it possible for her/his child to be as curious as possible. Curiosity doesn't thrive on a steady diet of "No" or constant imprisonment in a playpen.

Dale is curious about everything. He never stops, doesn't want anyone to pick him up. He's independent already. He has to see what everything feels like, what it looks like. He gets Cheerios, and loves to play with them. He pulls the drawers open and takes clothes out. He's trying to drink out of a cup, too.

Arlene, 17 - Dale, 11 months

Why is he so curious? Why does he have such a tremendous need to explore? Perhaps because he spent several months lying down, then sitting, but unable to move about. As he watched his world, he became more and more curious. Now that he's crawling, he can do something about his curiosity. He can explore. And explore he will.

You'll be amazed at the extent of his curiosity. He may turn the television on and off over and over again until you can stand it no longer. Think of the power he must feel when he pushes that button and the TV comes on!

He may open and shut a kitchen cupboard door dozens of times a day. If he finds paper on the floor, he'll crumple it. He'll investigate anything and everything.

Danette likes the wastebasket. She knocks it over and pounds on it. She opens the cupboard doors over and over and looks in. She'll stare, then grab something and walk away with it.

Caroline, 18 - Danette, 10 months

Robin swings doors back and forth. She smacks the bathroom door against the bathtub every morning and wakes my brother up. She'll do that for as long as she gets away with it.

Melinda

You'll probably see your baby staring intently at tiny particles. As she crawls across the floor, she'll pick up that speck of dust or the crumb she dropped from her high chair earlier. During this period, you may find yourself keeping your floors cleaner than you ever dreamed possible.

Not only will your baby notice every little thing on the floor . . . she'll also put it in her mouth. Her investigative urge is very strong. It's your job to see that she doesn't taste something that might hurt her.

Jay picks up fuzz balls off the floor, string, that one little thing is what catches his eye. He loves newspapers, loves tearing them up.

Bev, 17 - Jay, 8 months

Into-Everything Stage

Dale climbs up on the bed and on the couch, and he's trying to get on the table. I worry about him because he won't stay still at all, and I'm afraid he'll get into something. I watch him constantly.

Arlene

By the end of the first year, baby may be climbing. At first he will struggle to get on a low footstool. Soon he will master heights of a foot or so. If he can do that, he can climb on a chair. From there, he can climb to the table or to the kitchen counter. If you haven't baby-proofed your house and your habits, you now have a problem.

I worry about Robin all the time. She gets into everything, and she's on the go 24 hours a day. She falls and gets hurt because she tries to stand up on everything. She climbs on the couch. She climbs up me when I'm holding her in the rocking chair — she wants to climb up and look over the back.

Melinda

Has he learned to climb stairs? Then it's time to teach
him to come down safely. Show him how to slide down on
his stomach, feet first. Even if you have a gate on the stairs,
it may be left open occasionally, and he needs to learn.

Alice learned how to crawl up and down stairs
while we were in Texas, and she did it over and over.
At first, it scared me. She went up three stairs, and I
panicked and took her down. Then she started up
again and fell once. From then on, she could do it.

Melanie, 15 - Alice, 13 months

A one-year-old child is constantly active and constantly
moving. He's always completely absorbed in what he's
doing. He can be a fun companion because he is so active.
He can also be completely frustrating to you for the same
reason — he's so active.

Changing baby's diaper is quite a challenge during this
stage. Putting a toy in his hand may distract him from his
violent kicking and wriggling. You may even find you can
put a diaper on baby while he's standing up.

If all of this sounds as though baby is always in com-
mand, don't you believe it! Discipline is so important from
infancy on that *Discipline from Birth to Three* by Lindsay
and McCullough is devoted entirely to this subject.

Of course he'll try some things that must be stopped
with a "No." However, his understanding of "No," if he
hears it constantly, may be "Don't try" or "Don't find out."

He won't learn as he should if he decides he isn't supposed to explore, to try new things. But he can certainly
cope with the truly necessary "No."

Cruising and Walking

Alice isn't walking yet, but she takes a couple of
steps. She holds on to the couch and reaches, then

*goes from the couch to the table. She's been doing this
since she was about nine months old.*

Melanie

Soon after baby learns to stand, she may start cruising.
To cruise, she walks around while carefully supporting
herself by placing her hands on the couch, a chair, or some
other object.

A few babies go from crawling directly to walking. But
most cruise, sometimes for several weeks, even months. At
first she's extremely cautious, but before long she skims
along hand-over-hand the entire length of the couch.

She'd love to have you arrange your living room furniture so she can cruise all around the room. Set the furniture
close enough together to allow her to reach from one to
the other.

*Danette is walking. At about eight months, she
started walking around or to the furniture. She took
her first steps three or four weeks later. For a couple
of weeks, she just took a few steps; then she started
walking all over the place.*

Caroline

Walking at nine months is unusual. The average age to
start walking is between twelve and fourteen months. Some
children wait a couple of months longer.

First Physics Lesson

*Robin drops something from her high chair,
watches it drop, then screams for me to pick it up.
Then I tie it on a string so she doesn't hear it hit the
floor. Now she's learning to pick it up with the string.*

Melinda

Along about this time, while she's sitting in her high

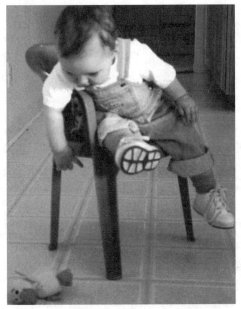

She can drop it, but she needs Mom or Dad to pick it up for her.

chair, baby will have her first physics lesson. She'll drop a spoon or a toy to the floor, then lean over to see what happened to it. This is serious learning on her part, and she'll try it again and again.

Of course mother or dad is supposed to hand the item back to her. Parents vary as to how long they're willing to continue this game. Most, however, will go along with it for awhile, especially when they realize it's a learning time for baby.

You can tie some toys to the high chair with a *short* (12 inches or less) heavy string. A longer string would be dangerous if she got it around her neck. Baby will learn to pull it back up herself. At first she won't be able to do that. She needs you to do it for her.

Supervision Needed Constantly

I worry about Maelynn getting hurt, but I try not to be overprotective. I worry about her falling down, but when she falls, I say, "Oh, oh, you fell." I don't make a big scene out of it.

I have an aunt who says, "Oh, did you get hurt? Oh no!" and this scares her kids more. I try to stay real calm so Maelynn won't get scared. I've watched my

cousins. After they fall, they keep playing until their
mother screams, then they start crying. I'm learning
a lot from them, and I don't want Maelynn to be
like them.

Joleen, 17 - Maelynn, 9 months

Your toddler requires even more constant supervision
than she did when she was crawling. She will run outside to
explore. By herself, she would run into a busy street. What
can you do about this? *Supervise her!* Try to be tolerant.
Remember how curious she is, and how impossible it is for
her to control her own actions at this age.

Your baby continues to like water play. Now that she's
older, this can be a problem if there is a pool nearby. A
child can drown in a couple of inches of water. *Always* be
with her when she's playing in water, whether it's in a tiny
pool or a big one, or even in a bathtub or a pail of water.

Keeping Baby Clean . . . Enough

Trying to keep an exploring toddler soap-and-water
clean at all times can upset her. It may also turn her into
a child who is afraid of getting dirty, which limits
drastically the amount of exploring she can do.

Buy or make the toughest and simplest clothes possible
for your little toddler. Make sure she doesn't feel guilty if
she gets herself and her clothes dirty. This is not a stay-
clean stage!

It's important, though, that you protect your child from
an overdose of harmful bacteria (germs).

While there are bacteria everywhere, most of them are
harmless. The body can cope with them. The body can also
cope with a few "bad" bacteria. But if these bad ones have
a good breeding place, they multiply rapidly. That's dangerous for baby. Good breeding grounds are food and feces.

Cooked food must be kept covered and cold or hot,

never warm. If a tiny bite of cream pie falls under the table and you miss it when you clean, bacteria will start multiplying. If baby picks that tiny piece of pie up several hours later and stuffs it in her mouth, it may make her very sick.

Be extra careful about cleanliness in the bathroom, too. Be sure you always wash your hands after you change her diaper. Wash her hands for her if she explores her own body while you change her. Mop up toilet accidents and burped-up milk quickly.

Always clean up pet feces immediately. This may mean inspecting your yard every morning, even several times a day, if your toddler plays there. Children can get pin worms and other diseases from handling pet feces.

Stranger Anxiety

Maelynn likes to play with people she knows, but she's afraid of other people. She'll smile at them, but when they come up to get her, she'll hug me and not let them pick her up. You can see she's afraid, but she won't cry if she knows I'm there. I explain to her, and she seems to understand.

Joleen

He still loves people — for awhile. But by about eight months of age, your friendly baby may suddenly refuse to look at strangers. Perhaps he won't even go to grandma. Has he turned into a frightened, timid child?

Not really. But he has matured enough to know exactly whom he trusts. He generally trusts the people he lives with and who take care of him most of the time. Now he doubts the others. Sometimes this is labeled "stranger anxiety."

Give baby time. If he hides his head in your shoulder as grandma holds out her arms to him, tell her he needs a few minutes to adjust. He'll go to her under his own terms.

Dependent on Mom

*I leave the room and Robin follows me because
she's so nosy. She wants to know where I'm going.
She'll follow me into the bathroom, and stand and
beat on the tub. You say "No" to her, and she'll give
you a real dirty look, then cry.*

*If somebody does something she doesn't like, she
will crawl over to me and want me to pick her up. She
doesn't just cry, she screams.*

Melinda

Toward the end of her first year, she may seem very
dependent on mother. She can't bear to see you leave. She
follows you all day long.

When you take her to visit a friend, she may spend the
entire time in your
arms. Only babies
with good attach-
ment to their moth-
ers act this way. It's
entirely normal, and
if she needs you, she
needs you.

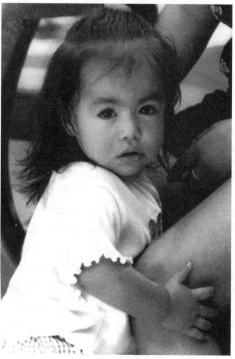

This clinging-to-
mother stage makes
it hard to leave baby.
It's not a good idea
to leave while she's
sleeping. When she
wakes up to find a
babysitter instead of
mother, she may be
very unhappy and
frightened. It's far
better to hire the

She sticks close to Mom.

sitter to come to your home a half-hour before you leave. Then baby has a better chance to adjust to the situation. If she cries as you leave, the sitter may report that she started playing happily by the time your car was out of sight.

As mentioned in chapter 3, playing peek-a-boo with baby from early infancy may help her realize if you go away, you come back. It takes time to understand that, if they leave, mother and dad really do come back.

Toilet-Teaching? Not Yet!

Toilet-training, really *teaching,* has not been mentioned in these chapters because most children aren't ready to use the toilet by themselves until they're past two years old. Some aren't ready until they're three.

Trying to toilet-teach a child before s/he's ready will most likely end in a lot of frustration for both of you. Unsuccessful toilet-teaching efforts, in fact, are probably one of the biggest problems leading to child abuse.

Don't be in a hurry. Wait until your child lets you know s/he is ready. See *Discipline from Birth to Three* for a helpful discussion of this subject.

Less Sleep Needed Now

Danette used to go to bed at 7 o'clock, but lately she's started going at 8:00. I give her supper. She plays for quite awhile, then at 8 o'clock I give her a bottle. After she drinks her bottle, she kisses me good night, and I put her to bed.

She's very very good about sleeping. She'll go to bed at 8:00, wake up next morning at 6:30. She has a bottle, then plays until 8:00 or 8:30. Then she wants her breakfast.

A couple of months ago she started fussing at bedtime. I wanted her to go to bed at a certain time,

so I would put her in her crib. She would cry, but I
would leave her in her crib for perhaps ten minutes.
That seemed like a long time, but she would get tired
and go to sleep. After two or three nights, she started
going to sleep right away.

Caroline

Your child needs less sleep as he grows older. By his
first birthday, he'll probably need only one nap per day.
Some babies want to nap in the morning. Then they get
fussy by mid-afternoon. If you put him down for a second
nap, he's awake later and later in the evening.

If you would like to have him in bed at a "decent" hour
at night, try keeping him awake a little longer in the morning. Then feed him a light lunch, perhaps at 10:30 a.m.,
before his nap. When he wakes two hours or so later, give
him another light lunch. He may last until early supper,
then go to bed for the night.

The morning nap can gradually be pushed to a later time.
Before long, he may be able to wait until noon for lunch,
then have his nap. This is important to a lot of parents.
Much as they love him, they like having their evenings free
of the constant child care they experience all day long.

Bedtime Routine Is Important

Many toddlers are not "very very good about sleeping."
Probably at least half put up some fuss about going to bed,
especially if other family members are still up.

Many parents prefer to have their small children in bed
two or three hours before they go to sleep themselves. Most
often a time between 6 p.m. and 8 p.m. is chosen. However,
a different schedule may work better for some parents.

Most important is that the child have a regular bedtime.
You can't keep her up until 10:00 tonight, then expect her

to lie down and go to sleep at 8 o'clock tomorrow night. Following the same routine every night helps most children accept bedtime.

Unless bathtime is a boisterous play session, bathing her before she goes to bed may relax her.

Does your baby have a favorite blanket or stuffed animal? Encourage her to take one special thing to bed with her. Most babies have a security blanket or other object that is important to them. Perhaps it's a loved teddy bear.

Attachment to the security object may begin in this eight-to-twelve month stage, although it will become much stronger later. Many mothers report that it's almost impossible to get that special blanket away from the child long enough to put it through the washing machine.

Help her find the blanket or teddy bear that is part of the going-to-bed ritual. Read her a story. Then breastfeed her or give her that last bottle of formula as you rock and sing or croon to her. It may take half an hour for her to unwind, to relax enough to go to sleep.

If she insists on taking her bottle to bed, remember the problem caused by formula dripping on her teeth all night. The milk film can cause serious tooth decay. If she insists on a bottle, you insist on putting water in it, not formula.

If you follow the same routine with your child every night, you may find she goes to bed fairly happily most of the time. Your evenings will be more pleasant, too, if putting your child to bed is not a struggle.

Soon your baby will celebrate her first birthday. No longer is she a tiny baby totally dependent on you for moving from room to room. She's awake, and she's extremely active much of the time. She's a busy little person.

Independent as she may appear at times, she still wants you nearby. You two have a good thing going as her attachment to you and love for you continues.

He's beginning to feed himself — and he loves it.

13

Time for Table Food

- **Big Changes
  in Eating**
- **Breastfeeding
  with Teeth?**
- **Weaning
  to a Cup**
- **When He Feeds
  Himself**
- **No Junk Food
  Here**
- **He's Messy!**
- **Food Is
  to Be Enjoyed**

*Haley eats baby food, cheerios,
table food. I smash the beans with
a little rice. I give her the soups
we eat, steamed potatoes, carrots,
broccoli.*

*She was seven months when she
started drinking from a cup. She
eats with us in the evening.*

*She plays with her food. She
smashes it, squeezes it.*

Shaquala, 17 - Haley, 9 months

*Makalah is starting to eat the
toddler food. She eats toast, little
pieces of vegetables. I cut them
real real small, like little potatoes.
I make sure they're real soft. I
smash carrots for her. She eats*

beans and rice, macaroni and cheese.
I'm starting to give her milk in a cup.

Nykesha, 16 - Makalah, 9 months

Alice won't eat out of a spoon. She refuses. She'll
pick it up and eat it with her fingers. She doesn't eat a
lot because I guess she's attached to the milk.
First I fed her fruits, bananas, and applesauce.
Then at eight months she went to real food. String
beans are her favorite.
She eats any kind of meat herself, turkey, chicken,
anything. She has ten teeth. She can chew the bone
from the chicken wing without my cutting off the meat.

Melanie, 15 - Alice 13 months

Dale is on table food. He doesn't much like eating
meat, but he likes vegetables. I don't have to mash
them. If I do, he gets mad because he can't pick them
up. He gets mad if I try to feed him, too, so I just put
food on his tray.

Arlene, 17 - Dale, 11 months

Big Changes in Eating

I've been nursing her, and I didn't start her on
solid food until she was six months old. I don't like
giving her stuff from cans, so I boil pears. I mash
bananas for her. She eats a lot of the things we
eat now.

Zandra, 16 - Dakota, 11 months

For the first four or five months of your baby's life,
eating meant breast or bottle. Babies do better without
added food during these early months.

By five or six months, she's ready for tiny amounts of
nearly liquid rice cereal and strained fruits and vegetables.

Most of her nutrition during this stage still comes from breast milk or formula. Those early solid foods are important mostly because she needs to learn to eat solids. Soon she'll need more than formula, and she needs time to learn this new method of eating.

From eight to twelve months, her eating pattern continues to change. No longer does she need her food blended with no lumps. Whether or not she has teeth, she can gum food after you've mashed it or it's gone through the baby food grinder.

Most babies need strictly smooth food, whether from a jar or food you prepare, only until they're about eight months old. By eight months you can chop and mash table foods for baby.

Of course baby's meals need to include the basic food groups just as yours do. Baby needs fruits and vegetables, whole grains, dairy foods, and protein. Fats and sweets should be limited for baby — and for us.

When you eat out, you might take a jar of Stage 2 or 3 fruits or vegetables for baby. Adding that to the hamburger and bun he'll be eating with you, plus formula, will give him a balanced meal.

Instead of the jar of baby food, you could take frozen "ice cubes" of his food from the freezer. (See page 145.) By the time you get to McDonalds, his special food will be thawed and ready to eat.

Is your baby taking vitamins? Even if you're breast-feeding, the doctor may prescribe vitamins by the time baby is a few months old.

It's important to keep mealtime pleasant. When baby refuses a food, don't push. Just offer it again in a couple of weeks. This is the time to help baby learn to enjoy a variety of foods. As his taste buds develop, he may relish something today that he couldn't stand last month.

She prefers to feed herself.

Amelia doesn't eat baby food any more. I nursed her for a long time without baby food, and people would say, "Oh, you should give her solid food."

I started rice cereal at about four months, but she didn't much like being fed like that. She has two teeth now, but she can chew anything. She can pretty much eat whatever she wants. I don't give her nuts, and she doesn't do well with strawberries — her cheeks get fiery red. I'm told they're a highly allergic food.

I don't buy baby food. I never fed her jarred meat. I think it's disgusting. I cut up chicken, steak, whatever we're eating. I cut it up good.

She loves yogurt and cottage cheese. Last night she ate a whole stick of string cheese. She drinks formula from a spouted cup.

I try to make it a balanced meal with fruit or vegetable, a grain, a protein.

Aimee, 17 - Amelia, 10 months

By the time he's eight months old, you'll be able to mash his food into small pieces. If you're serving chicken, get rid of the bone and cartilage. Then cut the meat into very small pieces for him.

Fish is excellent because it just falls apart. Of course, you have to be very careful to get all the bones out first.

> **Warning**
> Orange juice is not recommended until baby is about a year old. Some babies are allergic to it.

Many babies like cottage cheese. Just mash it with a fork.

Plain unflavored yogurt is good for baby. Don't choose the heavily sugared kind. Many children prefer the tart flavor of plain yogurt.

The above foods, along with formula or breast milk, can supply most of baby's vitamin and mineral needs. Iron fortified cereal can satisfy her need for iron. Fruits and vegetables, of course, are good sources of vitamins A and C.

Helping him learn to eat solid food is important. It's also very important that he continue getting plenty of breast milk or formula. He needs about twenty ounces each day now. Of course you don't know exactly how much he's getting from your breast, but if you're nursing him four times a day, and he seems satisfied and continues to be healthy and active, he's probably getting plenty.

Breastfeeding with Teeth?

Before Amelia had teeth, she turned her head all the way around once while she was nursing. I looked shocked and said, "No, Amelia, no. That hurts," and she didn't do it again.

Aimee

If you're breastfeeding, you may worry that when your baby has teeth, he'll bite you. Some people choose to switch to bottles at this point, but generally it won't be a problem. If baby bites your nipple, you'll respond, of course. As mentioned on page 121, if you say "No" *very* firmly and remove your nipple from his mouth for a couple of seconds, he's likely not to bite you again. Children at this age love this close breastfeeding time with mother.

Have you seen children who, at the age of one year or older, carried a bottle around with them? If you're bottle-feeding your child, and you'd rather not make weaning a hassle later, continue to hold him while he drinks his bottle. He'll get the loving closeness that breastfed babies cherish, and he'll not see his bottle as something that goes every-where with him — just as the breastfed baby can't have a breast to carry as he runs around.

Weaning to a Cup

If you're still breastfeeding her, you may decide to wean her directly to a cup in the next three or four months. If you haven't used bottles much, weaning will probably be easier for you if you let her go from your breast to the cup. Some babies are ready to drink enough milk from a cup by their first birthday. Others need to breastfeed a little longer.

Holding his own cup is an exciting development.

If she's bottle-fed, she still needs to learn to drink from a cup. She'll spill it, even try pouring it out, if you give her too much. With patience, she'll learn. Remember, she needs about twenty ounces of breast milk or formula daily, whether by cup, breast, and/or bottle.

A spouted "training" cup provides a bridge from sucking milk to learning to drink from a regular cup. It's also harder to spill or dump formula from a training cup.

Incidentally, babies should not be given regular milk until they're a year old. Skim or low-fat milk is not good for children under two years.

When He Feeds Himself

He's trying hard to use the spoon — doesn't quite have it yet. He puts his food on his spoon, but has trouble getting it to his mouth.

Arlene

When she's eating, she likes to get the spoon and bang it for awhile, then eat for awhile, then bang it again. She doesn't like me to feed her unless she's in a good mood. She likes to feed herself. She drinks by herself from a training cup, but she still takes a bottle.

Joleen, 17 - Maelynn, 9 months

If baby wants to help feed himself, let him. He won't be able to get much food to his mouth at first. He can put his hand on yours as you hold the spoon. Or he can have his own spoon while you get most of the food to his mouth with yours.

No Junk Food Here

Dalton's teeth are decayed now because we al-lowed him too much candy and pop, and he took the bottle for too long. He took it to bed with him. The

*milk stays on the teeth, and the sugar eats away at
them. If he woke up in the middle of the night, I'd pop
a bottle in his mouth, and we'd go back to sleep while
he sucked on his bottle.*

*I love soda, and any time I had some, he wanted it.
I didn't want to hear him scream, so I'd share it. Now
we don't have soda or candy in the house. It's not fair
to eat it in front of him. Trips to the dentist are no fun.*

Clair, 17 - Dalton, 33 months

Sometimes people try to pacify a child with a sweet treat
when a hug would work just as well. In fact, hugs are
always better than junk food. Jello water and other sweetened drinks are in the empty calorie category, too. Babies
and toddlers need formula or breast milk, water and unsweetened fruit juices to drink, *and seldom anything else.*

Coffee, tea, and cola drinks contain caffeine which is a
drug. Your baby doesn't need drugs.

You'll do him a real favor if you delay giving him junk
food — soda, candy, chips, etc. — as long as possible.
Your job is to help him learn to enjoy eating the foods he
needs to grow into a healthy, capable adult.

Not the First Year

Raw, crisp fruits and vegetables aren't good for
baby until past the first year because he might choke
on them. Until he's two, in fact, if you want him to
have raw carrots, you should grate them.

Corn is not for infants or toddlers. It goes right
through in the BM without changing color or shape.

Now is the time to help your baby grow into a pattern of
healthy eating that will continue throughout his life. Feeding him a variety of foods gives him an opportunity to
develop a taste for different foods.

He's Messy!

*Gilbert likes to feed himself, and he makes the
biggest mess. He eats mashed potatoes and string
beans. He has six teeth, and he can even chew on
meat already.*

Gaye, 15 - Gilbert, 7 months

A baby learning to feed himself is at his messiest. Don't
be shocked. Expect it and be prepared to cope with it.
Remember how much baby likes to explore, to touch, to
feel? That's exactly what he will do with his food. Some of
it will go in his mouth, but at first more seems to end up on
his face, in his hair, any place but where you'd like it to go.
He will be delighted with the whole mess. When he wants
to help, give him bits of toast or banana to hold while you
feed him. He may get some food to his mouth by smearing
it there with his palm.

The easiest way to feed him is to put him in a sturdy
high chair. When he starts feeding himself, lay newspapers
under the chair. A piece of heavy plastic protecting your
floor might look better than newspaper, but you don't want
something you have to clean. After each meal, just bundle
up the newspapers and throw them out.

Food Is to Be Enjoyed

Looking at, handling, tasting and smelling food is part of
the same exploring that begins earlier with inedibles. If he's
allowed to work out his own eating habits, he learns the
world is not a restrictive, forbidding place where showing
his own feelings and wants only brings trouble.

Keep cool and go along with his sheer enjoyment of the
whole eating process. This is the best route to making his
mealtimes the pleasant events you want them to be.

She's crusing now. Soon she'll be walking — then running.

14

Enjoying / Teaching Your Child

We sing patty-cake. We play with her and her toys, I sing to her. We get on the floor and play with her and with her toys. She's interested in everything.

She really likes the mirror. She sits there and hits it, and tries to talk.

Nykesha, 16 - Makalah, 9 months

I'm enjoying Danette more as the months go by — she gets better and better! I go crazy with her new toys. We sit on the rug and play all kinds of games. I bounce her up and down on the bed.

Danette likes music. She likes to sing. I hold her and dance with her a lot. I'm crazy with her.

We go outside, and I chase her all over. Jim and I
take her hands and run with her.
   I'll fill a can or a box with a bunch of stuff. She
likes to take one thing out at a time, play with it for
awhile, then take something else out and play with it.

                              Caroline, 18 - Danette, 10 months

A Great Time for Learning

As your child moves about, playing with him can be
even more fun for both of you. Not only is it fun, it's good
for his brain to interact a lot with you and other caregivers.
As discussed in Chapter 3, parents have a great deal to do
with their child's learning in his early months and years.

We know that a child who doesn't have a chance to learn
as he should during this stage may never catch up on that
missed learning. If no one talks much to a child, if his
parent is cold and distant, the child won't learn as well as
the child who interacts with loving parents and other
caregivers during much of his waking time. The more you
talk with your child, sing to/with him, read to him, cheer
him on, the brighter he'll be.

You can interact a lot with your child even as you do
other things. By this age, she probably doesn't want you
out of her sight. Does she protest if you go to the bathroom
without her? Remember, at this stage, when you vanish, she
feels deserted.

Parents who are okay with their child constantly following them around have a wonderful teaching opportunity. If
she's nearby as you work, you can talk to her. Tell her what
you're cooking. Let her help you dust the table.

You're her first and most important teacher, and you're
working far more than a 40-hour week with her. The sheer
magnitude of her learning at this point is mind-boggling.

Bronwyn lives with her mother, but she spends a lot of

time at her dad's house. Time with Dad is more learning
time for Bronwyn:

> *I take her on walks with the stroller. We sit in the*
> *backyard, and we play with my dog.*
> *I have a bucket full of toys, and I let her pick out*
> *the one she wants. If she hands me a toy, I sit and play*
> *with her. We talk a lot. She doesn't really talk yet, but I*
> *know she understands a lot. She's pretty amazing.*
>
> Brady, 17 - Bronwyn, 10 months

Most children this age love to play outdoors. If you don't
have a grassy yard, is there a park nearby? Of course, being
outside when you're not quite one year old means lots of
supervision from mother, dad, or another caregiver.

> *Dale loves being outside, and he likes the park a*
> *lot. We go every Sunday because his father plays*
> *baseball. We're constantly chasing after him.*
>
> Arlene, 17 - Dale, 11 months

Playing Together

Your child will love playing with you. Because she likes
to imitate, she may enjoy playing follow-the-leader. Keep it
simple at first. Clap your hands, put a hat on your head and
on hers, and wave your arms.

Sounds interest your toddler, just as they have since she
was an infant. Wind chimes outside her bedroom window
are pleasant for her. Records, radio, music boxes, and bells
will intrigue her. "Singing" with you is great fun.

> *Haley has a toy that makes music. She keeps time*
> *with the music. She moves her body and her feet like*
> *she's dancing.*
>
> Shaquala, 17 - Haley, 9 months

Dance with baby. Before she's standing or walking,
she'll love dancing in your arms. Later she'll entertain you

by dancing by herself.

Let her make her own "music" with a drum made from an empty oatmeal box. Tape the lid on the box, then give her a wooden spoon to use as a drum stick. Show her how to play her drum.

Early in this stage, baby will love to pull a toy on a string. When she's crawling, sometimes she'll go backward so she can watch the toy as she pulls the string. If the toy makes a noise as she pulls it, so much the better.

A favorite activity is emptying things. Your toddler will empty dresser drawers, kitchen cupboards, bookshelves, trash cans, whatever she can reach. As soon as you put things back, she'll be ready to take them out again.

I try to keep Dale out of cupboards. I put rubber bands on them. He pulls the drawers right out and takes clothes out. I tell him "No" and set him down, but he goes right back and does it again.

Arlene

Giving her a dresser drawer, a kitchen cupboard, and a bookshelf that are "hers" may help. Don't expect her to be satisfied only with emptying her toys, however. She'll like that kitchen cupboard a lot more if she can empty it of your pans and plastic containers. Of course you'll be sure all cleaning materials have been safely put away.

Amelia can get in the pots and pans in the kitchen and it's no big deal. I put them away when she's through. Some cupboards need to be locked, but I think kids should have at least the bottom drawer with things they can play with. Locking everything up wouldn't teach her anything.

Aimee, 17 - Amelia, 10 months

It may also help to give her a variety of containers to

empty. Perhaps her toys can be kept in small boxes or baskets. Giving her many opportunities to empty things "legally" should help her learn not to empty and re-empty everything else in the house.

Choosing Toys

Maelynn likes to play with her beach ball and a little tennis ball. She throws it, then wants someone to bring it back again.

Joleen, 17 - Maelynn, 9 months

Balls are the best toy of all for baby. He can roll them and throw them. Once he can crawl, he can go after the ball. Soon he'll enjoy a big beach ball as well as having a wonderful time with the smaller ones. Of course he likes it best if you play with him.

One-year-olds like giant snap-lock rings and beads. They're also ready for big wooden or plastic blocks. They play with them mostly by putting them in and dumping them out of containers. Your toddler may be able to balance one block on top of another soon.

Check your child's stuffed toys to be sure the eyes and ears are firmly attached. Does the animal have a bell around its neck or even a ribbon on which baby could choke? You need to take off any part of that toy that he could pull off.

A round cereal box makes a fine tunnel. Take the bottom off, then show baby how to push a car through his tunnel. He'll watch for his car at the other end. Or you can tie a string to the car, put the string through the tunnel, and let him pull the car through.

You can also make a cardboard hill for his car. Fold the cardboard to set at a slant on the floor. Then show baby how to put the car at the top of the hill and let it roll down.

Let her "help" you as much as possible as you work.

Let Him Help

Trying to copy what you do is important to a toddler. At eight months, he explores everything for the joy of exploring. Almost everything is new to him. A few months later, he wants to follow adults' examples. Earlier he banged with a spoon; now he will stir with it like mom does.

Baby loves to do what you do. Let him "help" you as much as possible as you do your work. While you're cooking, set him in his high chair near you. Are you baking a pie or making tortillas? Give him a little piece of dough so he can work along with you. If you're stirring something, give him a small pan and a spoon so he, too, can stir.

Interacting with Others

Busy as she is, your toddler will often show her affection for you and for others. Toward the end of her first year, she probably will like being around other children. She may play by herself, but she'll enjoy watching the others. Sometimes she may try to join their fun.

Don't expect a toddler to share her toys with another child for a long time yet. She's still too busy learning about herself and her world to be able to understand why Johnnie, just because he's a guest, should play with her ball.

Do you have an older child? If he's considerably older than the baby, he probably spends most of the time playing with children his age. When he does interact with the baby, he's probably quite gentle, and usually treats the baby like the baby she is.

A brother or sister not yet that mature, however, may show resentment and dislike for the baby. This stage is particularly difficult because the baby will constantly get into her brother's or sister's toys. She'll generally be a nuisance to your older toddler. The closer together the children are in age, the more hostile your older child may be.

As you supervise the two, remember that the older child, if he's under three, needs you almost as much as does the little one. You'll wonder at times how you can stretch your caring and your attention far enough for both.

Fusses between two toddlers are normal. A one-year-old and a two-year-old can't be expected to get along beautifully all the time, or even much of the time

More Language Development

Dale gets into everything. He's starting to talk, to say words. The other night I said "Good night," and he said "Night!" That's exciting.

Arlene

If you have talked to baby ever since he was born, and you've given him lots of learning experiences, he'll be working hard learning to talk by the end of his first year. He won't be saying many words yet, but he'll try. Researchers studied a group of mothers who read to their babies 15 to 20 minutes each day. They read from simple, inexpensive children's books, pointed at the pictures, and talked about them. They used the books as the basis for talking with their infants.

Language development of these children was compared with a carefully matched group of children whose mothers did not read to them consistently. By the time they were 17 months old, the children whose mothers had read to them had better speaking abilities than did the other group of children.

I read to Danette, especially Dr. Suess. I think reading to her gives her a head start in her education. I enjoy sitting and reading with her. I read mostly at night, but a lot of times in the afternoon, too, we'll read a book. Often I sit in my rocking chair, she sits on my lap, and we read.

Caroline

Playtime

Hide-and-seek can change. He may hide behind a chair and ask you to find him. He'll go into gales of giggling as you look behind each chair until you "find" the right one.

Maelynn likes to play choo-choo. She does it herself sometimes. She'll go behind something, then look out at me to surprise me, and I'll laugh.

She was trying to make me laugh the other day. She bumped her head lightly on the padded headboard. She didn't get hurt, and I laughed. So she did it again to make me laugh again.

Joleen, 17 - Maelynn, 9 months

Get on his level. Play on the floor with him when he learns to crawl. He'll love having you chase him all around the living room floor. Soon he may decide to chase you instead.

A small metal pan with a lid is a great toy, providing the lid has a rounded edge and isn't sharp. It takes patience and skill for baby to fit the lid on the pan. If you put a small object inside for a surprise, he'll be even more interested. After he has carefully examined the pan, you may need to show him how to take the lid off and put it back on.

You can also show him how a block sounds when you hit the pan with it. Show him the different sounds it makes when you tap his shoe with the block, then the floor. Noise is an important part of baby's life.

Water Play

Babies love water play. It can be relaxing for them, too. If you can't put baby outside with some water, perhaps you

He loves to play in the water.

Making Toys

Rice bags. Make him some small rice bags and show him how to throw them. Use a different textured fabric for each little bag, fur, satin, corduroy, and vinyl, for example. Simply cut two circles of fabric for each rice bag. With right sides together, sew tightly (preferably on a sewing machine) around the edge leaving a one-inch space for turning and stuffing. Turn right side out. Fill with rice. Sew up the hole with tiny stitches.

Using rice to stuff these little bags is far safer than using beans. He could choke on a bean. He could have a real problem if he stuffed a bean in his ear or nose. Don't risk it.

Feel-box. Use a box for the container. Put in a linoleum square, a playing card, big rubber sink stopper, and squares of different kinds of textured fabric.

Coffee can/clothespins toy. You can make a fine toy using a one-pound coffee can and the old-fashioned nonspring clothespins. Make sure the edge of the coffee can is smooth. Simply set the clothespins on the edge of the can. You might want to use a non-toxic paint to paint them red, yellow, and blue. You don't expect him to learn his colors yet, but you begin to introduce the idea of color when you say, "Let's put the red one on the can."

Drop the spool in the hole. A coffee can with a plastic lid can also be used for a "drop the spool in the hole" game. Cut a hole in the plastic coffee can lid a little bigger than the spools. Then show baby how to drop the spools into the can. Lids from frozen juice containers also work well as the drop-in toy.

can arrange it in your kitchen without too much trouble.
First, put down a good padding of newspapers, then
spread an old sheet over them. Put some water in a plastic
dish. One or two inches of water is enough. You want him
to splash, not flood the place. For added interest, you could
add food coloring or a little baby shampoo to the water.

For all water play, an *adult* must be present at all times.

You'll find he first splashes the water, tastes it, and has a
good time finding out all he can about it. You can add to his
fun by giving him a couple of ice cubes. Take them out
when they get so small he could choke if he put them in
his mouth.

When baby can sit up by himself, you'll probably bathe
him in the big bathtub. He'll love having a few floating
toys with him. Tell him to wash the fish's hair while you
wash his.

A plastic sieve for water play can be made from the
lower half of a plastic milk jug. Just poke holes in it with an
ice pick.

Make him a bath mitt with a washcloth. Cut two pieces
of cloth the shape and size of baby's hand. Sew them
together and, if you like, decorate them. Let him help wash
himself with his mitten. Of course you'll never turn your
back on him for a second while he's in the water.

Your Exciting Challenge

Loving, caring for, and guiding your child throughout
her early life is an exciting challenge. Your baby has become a "real" person, a child who is on her way to
becoming a self-sufficient individual.

You are an important part of her growth as you love her,
care for her, and enjoy games and activities with her.

Enjoy your time together.

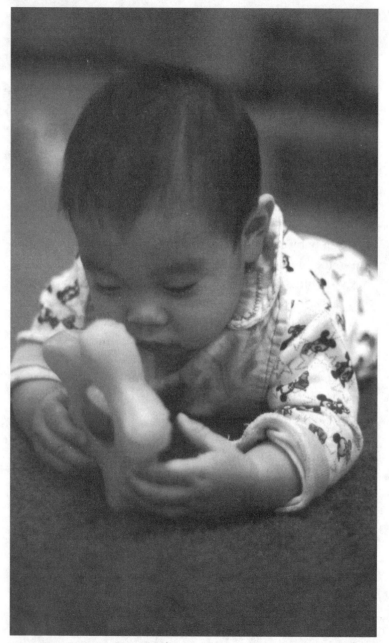

Mom has a wonderful incentive for working toward her goals.

15

Working Toward Your Future

My grandfather and my aunts were negative when I got pregnant. They said, "Oh, are you going to school? Why? You don't need that any more." The other day I told them I was working, and they made fun of me.

They think life is over for me. But I'll prove to them that I can do what I need to do even though I have a baby.

Shaquala, 17 - Haley, 9 months

It's harder being a single parent although Alice's father has been helping me. But he's too serious. He says within a year we should have this and that, and we'll get married. But I'm not going to

marry nobody.
This is what I want to do. I'm going to finish high
school in two years, I hope. Then I want to go to
nursing school. I don't want to be on welfare. I feel I
want to make my own money.

Melanie, 15 - Alice, 13 months

My future plans are to go back to school and get
my high school diploma. I need to do this because it's
a feeling I just can't shake off. It's like an itch I can't
scratch. I need to do it for my peace of mind.

Deborah, 16 - 7 months pregnant

Teen Parents and Poverty

A mother who has her first child before she is 18 is
likely to be poor during much of her life. Many young
mothers have found they must rely on welfare or minimum
wage for survival. Today, however, welfare reform seri-
ously limits the length of time a young mother qualifies for
this help.

A high percentage of the children born to teenage mothers grow up in poverty. However, according to research, it
doesn't seem to be the early parenting that causes the
poverty. *It's the lack of a good education and job skills.*
That lack, of course, often goes hand in hand with early
motherhood — and fatherhood.

Most young mothers of 15, or even 17, find it difficult to
continue their education. An obvious reason is the lack of
good and affordable child care in many areas. Even if a
grandmother is available for babysitting during the day, a
teenage mother will find high school life different and
usually harder than it is for her non-parenting friends.

For many young parents, it's too difficult. A majority of
the women in this country who deliver a child before 18
never finish their high school education.

Nearly half of all families headed by women live in poverty. Women without a high school education are more likely to head a family than are women who graduated. Yet these women with less education won't be able to earn as much as will their better-educated friends.

It seems ironic. If she doesn't have an education, she can't get a good job, and can't earn as much money. Yet she is more likely to be the sole wage earner for her family. Life isn't always fair.

Continuing School Is Crucial

Statistics show that if a young mother completes her education and doesn't have additional children right away, she may do as well as her friends who delay childbearing until later. If she becomes pregnant at an early age, gets married, drops out of school, and has more children rather quickly, she's likely to have money problems throughout her life.

High school mothers who get married are far more likely to drop out of school than are their single friends. Of those who are neither wives nor mothers, less than 10 percent drop out before finishing high school.

A higher percentage of unmarried teenagers who have a baby never graduate from high school. And even more of those who marry — a whopping 80 percent — quit school before they graduate.

These are factors you may be able to control. You start with your own situation. If you are a young parent with a child to support and care for, that's where you start with your life planning. If you aren't already married, you may decide to postpone your wedding. You may make sure you don't get pregnant again before you think you're ready for another baby. And you can do everything possible to continue your education.

I want to finish school for sure. It will be hard, but I've got to finish. Eventually I want to work with computers, but I'd like to stay home with the baby for awhile. At first I want a part-time job. Then when Racquelle starts school, I'll work full-time.

Cheryl, 15 - Racquelle, 2 months

Day Care Desperately Needed

Most young parents need day care services in order to complete their high school education. Day care isn't available for teenage parents in most school districts in the country.

Finding day care for her child is a serious problem for many young mothers. They need to continue their education, acquire job skills, and work in order to be self-supporting. To do this, they must have day care for their children. The lack of day care services condemns many young parents to reliance on welfare income for survival.

No longer, however, can a single mother depend on even the small welfare grant once available to single mothers who qualified. Welfare reform moved some of the decision-making on this issue to the states. The amount of time an individual qualifies for welfare support is now severely limited. For some teen parents, the challenge of supporting their family is overwhelming, especially if no one else in the family can care for their child.

Some young parents have a mother who is home at least part of the time. Alison's mother works, but is home by early afternoon. She is willing to take care of Stevie when she gets home, so Alison has planned a work schedule which will permit her to be home with her son during much of his waking time:

I'm going to look for a job soon as a hospital ward clerk. I'll try to get swing shift so I can be here most

of the day with Stevie. My mother comes home from
work by mid-afternoon. She could take care of Stevie
when I go to work.
He stays up late, so I could put him to bed when I
get home at 10 or 11 p.m. I'd like to be able to
do that.

Alison, 18 - Stevie, 2 months

If Relatives Can't Help

Many grandparents, of course, are not available for
babysitting. In the first place, they may not want to care for
a child. Perhaps your mother feels she has raised her family
and she doesn't want to start over again. You can probably
understand her feelings.

Even if she's willing to baby-sit, grandma may have a
job herself. Everyone in your family may already be working. There may be no one at home who will/can take care
of your baby for you.

Some schools have infant care on campus.

*I do most of the caregiving. I take her to school
because they started a daycare this semester. It's a
real help. My mom goes to work, and I didn't know
what I was going to do*

                                        Alaina, 17 - Caelin, 4 months

Unless you're one of the lucky few teenage parents in
this country whose school offers child care for its students'
babies, you have a real problem. You know how important
it is to continue your education. Perhaps you've finished
high school, but you want to get further job training or go
on to college. You may be ready to get a job now, and you
don't want to settle for staying home and living on aid even
if you might qualify for a short time.

Who will care for your child while you're in school or
working?

Most day care centers are for children who are at least
two years old. Many will only accept children who are
toilet-trained. Your community may not even have a
childcare center which takes babies and toddlers. To find
out, check with your school district and family service
agencies.

Family day care may be available. In this arrangement, a
person cares for a small number of children in her/his own
home. Some day care homes are licensed, some are not.

In order to provide good day care, one person should be
responsible for no more than five children including her/his
own. No more than two of these children should be under
two years of age.

If you can afford it, you might prefer to find a caregiver
who will come to your home to care for your child. Babies
and toddlers aren't likely to want the same schedule as you
must follow. Being able to let your child sleep while you go
on to school could be good for both of you.

Choosing a Caregiver

The decision you make about day care for your child is extremely important. Yet some people appear to put less thought into selecting a caregiver for their child than they do in buying a car! Whether you choose a day care center, family day care, or a caregiver who comes to your home, be sure you put a lot of thought into your choice.

Ask questions, lots of them. Don't hire the first person you find. Talk to several caregivers, then choose the one you think would be best for your child. One mother described her search for a caregiver for her small son:

I started answering other people's ads in our local paper. Then I ran an ad myself, and that was how I met the best ones.

When people called me, I would ask them a bunch of questions. I could tell from that first telephone conversation that I didn't want some of them. I interviewed at least twenty people before I decided.

I had lots of questions:

• *How many kids do you care for?*

• *How old are they?*

• *How do you discipline children?*

• *What do you do when a baby cries?*

• *When my son starts crawling, how will you protect your house? What about child-proofing? (If she said she used a playpen, she was off my list.)*

If I liked what she said on the phone, I would visit her, preferably without a lot of advance notice. I wanted to see what her house was like, how she coped. If she cared for other kids, I would try to visit while they were there.

Her school district provides child care and transportation.

Of course I wanted to be sure she had a place for Bryan to eat, to sleep, to play. What kinds of activities would she have for toddlers? I asked all sorts of questions.

Tricia, 18 - Bryan, 6 months

Remember, you're the employer when you hire a caregiver. You're the one making the decision. You have the right to ask about anything that might have something to do with your child's welfare. Ideally, you'll be able to find someone who will care for and love your child in much the same way as you do when you're with him.

Before you make your selection, be sure to ask if the caregiver takes care of sick children. If she doesn't, perhaps you have a friend or someone in your family who is willing to be on call for babysitting during minor illnesses. Babies and children get sick at inconvenient times.

Once you find a caregiver, will you continue checking

on the kind of care your child is receiving? If he isn't talking yet, he can't tell you what is going on when you're gone. Even if he's older, you need to know as much as possible about his "other home." You could make excuses to visit your child occasionally at unexpected times. This is one way to learn about the kind of care he's receiving. A good caregiver should welcome your interest and concern.

Paying for Child Care

Finding child care is one thing. Paying for it is another. If you qualify for TANF (Temporary Aid for Needy Families), talk to your social worker. There may be extra money available for child care while you continue your education or learn job skills. Or you might qualify for a child care grant through your local college. You can probably find out by contacting the women's center at the college.

If you're on welfare, perhaps you could get into a program that provides assistance with on-the-job training. Such a program might provide extra help with child care, transportation, and other job-related expenses while you're in school or in job training.

If you can't afford to pay a caregiver, and you have no one who will take care of your child at no charge, can you trade child care duties with another young parent? It would be hard to make such an arrangement work if you need to attend high school full-time.

If you're interested in attending night school, or if you're a college student, a trade might work. Schedule your classes so you can care for the other child while her mother is in class. Then she can be responsible for yours while you go to school. Caring for two children while you're trying to study would be difficult. It could be a way, however, to get that education you need so badly for your child's sake as well as your own.

Planning Your Family

I'm going to have two children at the most. I think two is enough. I think ideally I would have another one when Dale's about three when he more or less does things on his own.

Arlene, 17 - Dale, 11 months

Many teen mothers and fathers who have one child are able to continue their education and work toward their goals.

If they have a second child before they have finished school, the difficulties multiply. Having more than one child limits one's independence drastically:

It's really hard — a second kid seems like five more. I guess I shouldn't have had her. I tell Charles, "You were right. I should have had an abortion." I wanted to get everything over with — graduate, get my license, have the two kids. But now I don't really have anything. I'm tired and nervous and crabby.

Colleen 18 - Ruby, 7 months; Hilda, 21 months

The money cost of having a second baby soon after the first can be overwhelming:

You don't think the expense of a second baby is that much, but it is. It costs a lot more with Ruby. Charles used to work overtime last year for extras like Christmas. Now he has to work overtime so we can make it through the month.

Maybe it wouldn't be so bad if we were living in a house and had a lot of things, then said, "We're broke." But it shouldn't happen when we're in a one-bedroom apartment. You wouldn't believe what it costs for these two kids.

Colleen

From baby's standpoint, waiting three or even four years before the next child is wise. A two-year-old needs about as much care, in different ways, as does an infant.

When we brought Leon home from the hospital, DeeDee was three. She wanted to hold him, so we set her down on the couch and propped a pillow on her so she could. Ever since, he's been her baby. We've had very little jealousy.

If we had had him sooner, DeeDee couldn't have enjoyed being a baby long enough. I wanted her to be a little more independent so she would be used to me not spending so much time with her.

A lot of mothers I've seen have their kids real close together. It kind of makes the oldest child feel neglected. The little baby has to grow up so fast instead of enjoying being a baby.

Tamera, 21 - Leon, 10 months; DeeDee, 4 years

Babies do come by accident. If you don't want another child right away, birth control is essential. This could be simply not having intercourse, but most parents will want some other kind of contraceptive. If you're breastfeeding, don't count on it to keep you from getting pregnant. You can get pregnant even though you're breastfeeding.

If you're breastfeeding, check with your doctor about taking the birth control pill. Some pills are likely to cut down on your milk supply. It might be better to choose another contraceptive while you're breastfeeding.

This might be a good time to ask your doctor about inserting an IUD (<u>intrau</u>terine <u>d</u>evice). Or you might consider the contraceptive implant, the patch, or an every-three-months injectible such as Depo Provera. Check with your healthcare provider.

If the man uses a condom (rubber) and the woman uses

foam, the two methods together are as successful at preventing conception as is the pill or the IUD. Both the condom and foam can be bought at a drugstore with no prescription from the doctor.

Nykesha perfers the contraceptive patch:

> *I'm not sure I want another baby — maybe sometime when I'm out of my mom's house.*
>
> *I'm using the patch because it's so easy. You put one on for a week, take it off, put another one on, and do the same thing the third time. After three weeks you take it off for a week.*

For more information on birth control methods, see *Your Pregnancy and Newborn Journey* by Lindsay and Brunelli.

Sexually active couples need to discuss their thinking concerning contraception. If this is difficult for you, remember that having another baby too soon would also be hard on your partner. Brad talked about this issue:

> *I'd rather have three years between children. I want my first son to have time for me to teach him.*
>
> *How to talk about sex? First of all, be alone. Ask her how she feels about using protection. How many kids do you want to have? If one or the other doesn't want to use protection, they have to talk it through.*
>
> Brad, 17 - Adam, 13 months

If you aren't pregnant now, and you don't want to have a child soon, you have two choices. One, of course, is not to have sex. If you're having sex, use birth control — always.

Your Long-Range Goals

Long-range goals are important too. Where do you want to be in five years? The problem with long-range goals, however, is that they're too easy. You might say, "In five years, I'll be out of school, married, and living in a big house. We'll have another baby. Doug will be working, and I'll stay home with the children."

That's a long-range goal, and if this is what you want, by all means continue planning and working toward it.

Most important, what are you doing this year, *this month,* to work toward the life you want for yourself and your child? What must you do in order to continue your education? What steps can you take *now* to begin or continue your job skills training?

Right now I'm paying attention to school. I'll graduate next spring. My goal is to keep studying, go on to college. I don't put limits on my life. If you want something, you need to do whatever you can to reach that goal.

Right now, they're saying I won't graduate because I have a daughter. I'm going to show them.

Kimiko, 17 - Sujatha, 5 months

If you and your baby's other parent are together, you both need to continue your education and job skills training — unless, of course, one or both of you is job-ready now.

Sometimes young mothers still think they won't have to get a job because their baby's father will support them. For most of us, this is not a realistic expectation for several reasons:

- Many two-parent families find both parents must work to support their family.

- The majority of teenage marriages end in a short time.

- As a parent, you need to be educated in order to be the best possible parent to your child.

What are you doing today to make a satisfying future for yourself and your child?

Appendix

About the Author

Jeanne Warren Lindsay is the author of sixteen books for and about pregnant and parenting teens. Almost 700,000 copies of her books had been sold by 2004.

Lindsay's books deal with teenage pregnancy, parenting, adoption from the birthfamily's perspective, and teen relationships. Her *Teen Dads: Rights, Responsibilities and Joys* was selected by the American Library Association as a Recommended Book for Reluctant Young Adult Readers.

Lindsay has worked with hundreds of pregnant and parenting teenagers. She developed the Teen Parent Program at Tracy High School, Cerritos, California, and coordinated the program for many years. Most of her books are written for pregnant and parenting teens, and quotes from interviewees are frequently used to illustrate concepts.

Lindsay grew up on a farm in Kansas. She has lived in the same house in Buena Park, California, for 43 years. She loves to visit the Middle West, but says she's now addicted to life in southern California. She and her husband, Bob, have five children and seven grandchildren.

Lindsay is the editor of *PPT Express*, a quarterly newsletter for teachers and others working with pregnant and parenting teens. She speaks frequently at conferences across the country, but says she is happiest while interviewing young people for her books or writing under the big elm tree in her backyard.

Bibliography

The following bibliography contains books of interest to pregnant and parenting teens. Workbooks and other classroom aids are available for some of these titles.

Prices quoted are from late 2003. Because prices change so rapidly, however, call your local or internet book store or your local library reference department for an updated price and address before ordering a book. If you can't find a book in your local or internet bookstore, you can usually get it directly from the publisher. Enclose $3 for shipping per book. See page 2 3 for an order form for Morning Glory Press publications.

Anasar, Eleanor. **"You and Your Baby: Playing and Learning Together." "You and Your Baby: A Special Relationship."** 2001. **"You and Your Baby: The Toddler Years."** 2003. 32 pp. each. Each available in Spanish edition. $2.65 each. Bulk discounts. The Corner Health Center, 47 North Huron Street, Ypsilanti, MI 48197. 734.484.3600.
Gorgeous photos of teen parents and their children on every other page. Each booklet contains helpful information at an extremely easy reading level.

Arnoldi, Katherine. *The Amazing True Story of a Teenage Single Mom.* 1998. 176 pp. $16. Hyperion.
Written in a true experience/comic book format, it's the story of a young mom who had dreams, but faced many obstacles in fulfilling them.

Beaglehole, Ruth. *Mama, listen! Raising a Child without Violence: A Handbook for Teen Parents.* 1998. 224 pp. $25. Curriculum Guide, $20. Ruth Beaglehole, 2162 Echo Park Ave., Los Angeles, CA 90026. 323.661.9123.
A unique book. Most of it is written as if a toddler is speaking, explaining what s/he needs from his/her parents. Good description of emotional needs of small children. An absolute lack of violence (no spanking) is recommended throughout.

Brinkley, Ginny, and Sherry Sampson. *You and Your New Baby — A Book for Young Mothers.* Also in Spanish: *Usted y su nuevo bebé.* 1996. 80 pp. $3. ICEA, P.O. Box 20048. 951.854.8660.
Simple guide for teenage parents concerning caring for baby. Written in a format for easy understanding.

Gottfried, Ted. *Teen Fathers Today.* 2001. $24.90. Twenty First Century Books.
Focuses on teen fathers in America and their role in the childrearing process. Real-life stories complement the discussions. Provides practical information such as dealing with the reactions of parents, realities of pregnancy and birth, and taking responsibility for one's baby.

Harris, Robie H. Illus. by Michael Emberley. *It's Perfectly Normal: Changing Bodies, Growing Up, Sex and Sexual Health.* 1996. 89 pp. $10.99. Candlewick Press.
The illustrations are wonderful, and make it difficult to continue thinking of sex as something we never talk about with our children.

Jacobs, Thomas A., et al. *What Are My Rights? 95 Questions and Answers about Teens and the Law.* 1997. 208 pp. $14.95. Free Spirit Publishing. 612.338.2068.
A matter-of-fact guide to the laws that affect teens at home, at school, on the job, and in their communities.

Lansky, Vickie. *Feed Me — I'm Yours.* 1994. 141 pp. $9. Meadowbrook, Inc., 18318 Minnetonka Boulevard, Deephaven, MN 55391. 800.338.2232.
An excellent cookbook for new parents. Lots of recipes for making baby food "from scratch." Also includes directions for kitchen crafts.

_____. ***Games Babies Play from Birth to Twelve Months.*** 1993. 112 pp. $8.95. The Book Peddlers, 15245 Minnetonka Boulevard, Deephaven, MN 55345-1510. 800.255.3379.
Collection of activities — 20-30 ideas for each three months of the first year. Assign several activities each week to students for interacting with their babies as part of your ages and stages curriculum.

Leach, Penelope. ***Your Baby and Child from Birth to Age Five.*** Revised, 1997. 560 pp. $20. Alfred A. Knopf.
An absolutely beautiful book packed with information, many color photos and lovely drawings. Comprehensive, authoritative, and outstandingly sensitive guide to child care and development.

Lieberman, E. James, M.D., and Karen Lieberman Troccoli, M.P.H. ***Like It Is: A Teen Sex Guide.*** 1998. 216 pp. $25. McFarland and Co.
Excellent book to offer teen parents (all teens actually). It describes methods of contraception, starting with abstinence, and the risks associated with each one. Gives bias-free information about pregnancy options.

Lindsay, Jeanne Warren. ***The Challenge of Toddlers*** and ***Your Baby's First Year (Teens Parenting*** Series). 2004. 224 pp. each. Paper, $12.95 each; hardcover, $18.95 each. Workbooks, $2.50. Quantity discounts. Morning Glory Press. 888.612.8254.
How-to-parent books especially for teenage parents. Lots of quotes from teenage parents who share their experiences. Board games ($29.95 each), one for each of these titles, provide great learning reinforcement. Also see video series, **Your Baby's First Year.** *For detailed teaching guides, see* **Challenge of Toddlers** *and* **Nurturing Your Newborn/Your Baby's First Year Comprehensive Curriculum Notebooks.**

_____. ***Do I Have a Daddy? A Story About a Single-Parent Child.*** 2000. 48 pp. Paper, $7.95; hardcover, $14.95. Free study guide. Morning Glory Press.
A beautiful full-color picture book for the child who has never met his/her father. A special sixteen-page section offers suggestions to single mothers.

_____. ***Pregnant? Adoption Is an Option.*** 1996. 224 pp. $11.95. Teacher's Guide, Study Guide, $2.50 each. Morning Glory Press.
Birthparents share stories of responsible, difficult adoption planning. Does not "push" adoption, but suggests **planning** *and deliberate decision-making. Stresses open adoption and birthparents' role in choosing adoptive parents.*

_____. ***Teenage Couples — Caring, Commitment and Change: How to Build a Relationship that Lasts. Teenage Couples — Coping with Reality: Dealing with Money, In-laws, Babies and Other Details of Daily Life.*** 1995. 208, 192 pp. Paper, $9.95 ea.;

hardcover, $15.95 ea. Workbooks, $2.50 ea. Curriculum Guide, $19.95. Morning Glory Press.
Series covers such important topics as communication, handling arguments, keeping romance alive, sex in a relationship, jealousy, alcohol and drug addiction, partner abuse, and divorce, as well as the practical details of living. Lots of quotes from teenage couples.

_____. **Teen Dads: Rights, Responsibilities and Joys (Teens Parenting Series)**. 2001. 224 pp. $12.95. Workbook, $2.50. Morning Glory Press.
A how-to-parent book especially for teenage fathers. Offers help in parenting from conception to age 3 of the child. Many quotes from and photos of teen fathers. For detailed teaching help, see **Teen Dads Comprehensive Curriculum Notebook.**

_____ and Jean Brunelli. **Nurturing Your Newborn: Young Parent's Guide to Baby's First Month. (Teens Parenting Series)** 1999. 96 pp. $6.95. Workbook, $2. Quantity discounts. Morning Glory Press.
Focuses on the postpartum period. Ideal for teen parents home after delivery. For detailed teaching help, see **Nurturing Your Newborn/Your Baby's First Year Comprehensive Curriculum Notebook.**

_____, _____ . **Your Pregnancy and Newborn Journey (Teens Parenting Series)**. 2004. 224 pp. Paper, $12.95; hardcover, $18.95; Workbook, $2.50. Morning Glory Press.
Prenatal health book for pregnant teens. Includes section on care of newborn and chapter for fathers. For detailed teaching help, see **Your Pregnancy and Newborn Journey Comprehensive Curriculum Notebook.** Also see **Pregnancy and Newborn Journey board game** and **Pregnancy Two-in-One Bingo game**.

_____ and Sally McCullough. **Discipline from Birth to Three**. 2004. 224 pp. Paper, $12.95; hardcover, $18.95. Workbook, $2.50. Quantity discounts. Morning Glory Press.
Provides teenage parents with guidelines to help prevent discipline problems with children, and for dealing with problems when they occur. For detailed teaching help, see **Discipline from Birth to Three Comprehensive Curriculum Notebook.** *Also see four-video series,* **Discipline from Birth to Three.**

Marecek, Mary. **Breaking Free from Partner Abuse.** 1999. 96 pp. $8.95. Quantity discount. Morning Glory Press.
Lovely edition illustrated by Jami Moffett. Underlying message is that the reader does not deserve to be hit. Simply written. Can help a young woman escape an abusive relationship.

McCoy, Kathy, Ph.D., and Charles Wibbelsman. ***Teenage Body Book Guide.*** 1999. 288 pp. $18.95. Perigee Publishing.
Crammed with information for teenagers about everything from their bodies, changing feelings, teenage beauty, and special medical needs of young adults to sexuality, venereal disease, birth control, pregnancy and parenthood. Lots of quotes from young people, sometimes in the form of questions.

MELD Parenting Materials. **Nueva Familia.** Six books, each in Spanish and English editions. ***Baby Is Here. Feeding Your Child, 5 months-2 years. Healthy Child, Sick Child. Safe Child and Emergencies. Baby Grows. Baby Plays.*** 1992. $12 each. MELD, Suite 507, 123 North Third Street, Minneapolis, MN 55401. 612.332.7563.
Very easy to read books full of information. Designed especially for Mexican and Mexican American families, but excellent for anyone with limited reading skills. Ask MELD for catalog of other materials designed especially for school-age parents.

_____. ***The New Middle of the Night Book: Answers to Young Parents' Questions When No One Is Around.*** 1999. 163 pp. $12.50. MELD.
Includes clearly written information about parenting during the first two years of life. An especially good section discusses the benefits and how-tos of shared parenting, whether or not the parents are together as a couple.

Parent Express Series: ***Parent Express: For You and Your Infant.*** *Spanish edition:* ***Noticlas para los padres. Parent Express: For You and Your Toddler.*** Each newsletter, 8 pp. $4 each set. ANR Publications, University of California, 6701 San Pablo Avenue, Oakland, CA 94608-1239. 510.642.2431.
Wonderful series of newsletters for parents. The first set starts two months before delivery and continues monthly through the first year of the child's life. Second set with twelve letters covers second and third years. Good resource for teen parents. Beautiful photos, easy reading.

Pollock, Sudie. ***Will the Dollars Stretch? Teen Parents Living on Their Own.*** 2001. 112 pp. $7.95. Teacher's Guide, $2.50. Morning Glory.
Five short stories about teen parents moving out on their own. As students read, they will get the feel of poverty as experienced by many teen parents — as they write checks and balance checkbooks of young parents involved.

_____. ***Moving On: Finding Information You Need for Living on Your Own.*** 2001. 48 pp. $4.95. 25/$75. Morning Glory Press.
Fill-in guide to help young persons find information about their community, information needed for living away from parents.

Porter, Connie. *Imani All Mine*. 1999. 218 pp. $12. Houghton Miflin.
*Wonderful novel about a black teen mom in the ghetto where poverty,
racism, and danger are constant realities.*

Renfrew, Mary, Chloe Fisher, and Suzanne Arms. *Bestfeeding: Getting
Breastfeeding Right for You*. 1995. 240 pp. $14.95. Celestial Arts
Publishing, P.O. Box 7123, Berkeley, CA 94707. 800/841-2665.
*Marvelous description, with lots of photographs and drawings (150+) of the
importance of breastfeeding, and of how to make the process work.
Wonderful resource for teacher. While many students may not want to read
the whole book, simply looking at the photos and drawings could be helpful.*

Reynolds, Marilyn. **True-to-Life Series from Hamilton High.** *Baby
Help. Beyond Dreams. But What About Me? Detour for Emmy.
Telling. Too Soon for Jeff, Love Rules, If You Loved Me*. 1993-
2001. 160-256 pp. Paper, $8.95 each (*Love Rules*, $9.95). Morning
Glory Press.
*Wonderfully gripping stories about situations faced by teens. Start with
Detour for Emmy, award-winning novel about a 15-year-old mother.
Students who read one of Reynolds' novels usually ask for more. Topics
cover partner abuse, acquaintance rape, reluctant teen father, sexual
molestation, racism, fatal accident, abstinence, homophobia, school failure.*

Seward, Angela. Illustrated by Donna Ferreiro. *Goodnight, Daddy*.
2001. 48 pp. Paper, $7.95; hardcover, $14.95. Morning Glory Press.
*Beautiful full-color picture book shows Phoebe's excitement because of her
father's visit today. She is devastated when he calls to say, "Something has
come up." Book illustrates the importance of father in the life of his child.*

Silberg, Jackie. *125 Brain Games for Babies*. 1999. 143 pp. $14.95.
Consortium Book Sales. *125 Brain Games for Toddlers and Twos*.
2000. $14.95. Gryphon House.
*Packed with everyday games, songs, and other opportunities to encourage
the brain development of children from birth through three years. Illus.*

Wiggins, Pamela K. *Why Should I Nurse My Baby?* 1998. 58 pp.
$5.95. Noodle Soup, 4614 Prospect Avenue, #328, Cleveland, OH
44103. 216.881.5151.
*Easy-to-read, yet thorough discussion of breastfeeding. Question and
answer format. Also ask about the **Babies First** pamphlets, same source.*

Wolff, Virginia E. *Make Lemonade*. 2003. 208 pp. $5.99. Scholastic.
*Wonderful novel about a teenager living in a Project who takes a job
babysitting for a teenage mom, and who eventually sees the mom back in
school, her children in child care, and her life back on focus.*

Index

ORDER FORM — Page 1
Morning Glory Press
6595 San Haroldo Way, Buena Park, CA 90620
714.828.1998; 888.612.8254   Fax 714.828.2049
Contact us for complete catalog including quantity and other discounts.

		Price	Total

__ *Complete* **Teens Parenting Curriculum** $1085.00   _____

One each — Five *Comprehensive Curriculum Notebooks*
plus 8 books, 6 workbooks, 8 videos, 4 games
(everything on this order form except last 13 titles as noted on p. 2)
Buy a text and workbook for each student.
Contact us for generous quantity discounts.

Resources for Teen Parent Teachers/Counselors:
Books, Babies and School-Age Parents

Books, Babies and School-Age Parents	1-885356-22-6	14.95	_____
__ *ROAD to Fatherhood*	1-885356-92-7	14.95	_____

Resources for Teen Parents:
Your Pregnancy and Newborn Journey

Title	ISBN	Price	Total
Paper	1-932538-00-3	12.95	_____
Hardcover	1-932538-01-1	18.95	_____
Workbook	1-932538-02-x	2.50	_____
__ *PNJ Curriculum Notebook*	1-885356-96-x	125.00	_____
__ **PNJ Board Game**	1-885356-19-6	29.95	_____
__ **Pregnancy Two-in-One Bingo**	1-885356-64-1	19.95	_____
__ *Nurturing Your Newborn*	1-885356-58-7	6.95	_____
Workbook	1-885356-61-7	2.00	_____

Your Baby's First Year

Title	ISBN	Price	Total
Paper	1-932538-03-8	12.95	_____
Hardcover	1-932538-04-6	18.95	_____
Workbook	1-932538-05-4	2.50	_____
__ *BFY/NN Curriculum Notebook*	1-885356-97-8	125.00	_____

Four-video series — Your Baby's First Year

Title	ISBN	Price	Total
Nurturing Your Newborn	1-885356-86-2	69.95	_____
She's Much More Active	1-885356-87-0	69.95	_____
Leaving Baby Stage Behind	1-885356-88-9	69.95	_____
Keeping Your Baby Healthy	1-885356-89-7	69.95	_____
__ **All Four Videos — Baby's First Year Series**		195.00	_____
__ **Baby's First Year Board Game**	1-885356-20-x	29.95	_____

Four-video series — Discipline from Birth to Three

Title	ISBN	Price	Total
Infants and Discipline	1-885356-82-x	69.95	_____
He's Crawling — Help!	1-885356-83-8	69.95	_____
She's into Everything!	1-885356-84-6	69.95	_____
Your Busy Runabout	1-885356-85-4	69.95	_____
__ **All Four Videos — Discipline Birth to Three Series**		195.00	_____

SUB-TOTAL (Carry over to top of next page)   _____

SUB-TOTAL FROM PREVIOUS PAGE _____

More Resources for Teen Parents:

Discipline from Birth to Three

—	Paper	1-932538-09-7	12.95 _____
—	Hardcover	1-932538-10-0	18.95 _____
—	Workbook	1-932538-11-9	2.50 _____
__ *Discipline Curriculum Notebook*		1-885356-99-4	125.00 _____

The Challenge of Toddlers

—	Paper	1-932538-06-2	12.95 _____
—	Hardcover	1-932538-07-0	18.95 _____
—	Workbook	1-932538-08-9	2.50 _____
__ *CT Curriculum Notebook*		1-885356-98-6	125.00 _____
__ **Challenge of Toddlers Bd. Game**		1-885356-56-0	29.95 _____

Teen Dads: Rights, Responsibilities and Joys

—	Paper	1-885356-68-4	12.95 _____
—	Workbook	1-885356-69-2	2.50 _____
__ *Teen Dads Curriculum Notebook*		1-885356-95-1	125.00 _____

Following books are NOT included in Complete *Teens Parenting* Curriculum:

__ *Do I Have a Daddy?* Paper	0-885356-63-3	7.95 _____
__ *Pregnant? Adoption Is an Option*	1-885356-08-0	11.95 _____
__ *Surviving Teen Pregnancy*	1-885356-06-4	11.95 _____
__ *Teenage Couples: Caring, Commitment and Change*		
—	0-930934-93-8	9.95 _____
— *Teenage Couples: Coping with Reality*	0-930934-86-5	9.95 _____

Novels by Marilyn Reynolds:

__ *Love Rules*	1-885356-76-5	9.95 _____
__ *If You Loved Me*	1-885356-55-2	8.95 _____
__ *Baby Help*	1-885356-27-7	8.95 _____
__ *But What About Me?*	1-885356-10-2	8.95 _____
__ *Too Soon for Jeff*	0-930934-91-1	8.95 _____
__ *Detour for Emmy*	0-930934-76-8	8.95 _____
__ *Telling*	1-885356-03-x	8.95 _____
__ *Beyond Dreams*	1-885356-00-5	8.95 _____

TOTAL _____

Add postage: 10% of total—Min., $3.50; 15%, Canada _____
California residents add 7.75% sales tax _____

TOTAL _____

Ask about quantity discounts, teacher, student guides.
Prepayment requested. School/library purchase orders accepted.
If not satisfied, return in 15 days for refund.

NAME _____

PHONE_____ Purchase Order #_____

ADDRESS _____
_____